TEST SMART!

◆ ◆ ◆ ◆ ◆

Ready-to-Use Test-Taking Strategies and Activities for Grades 5-12

GARY W. ABBAMONT

ANTOINETTE BRESCHER

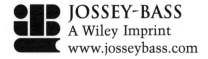

JOSSEY-BASS
A Wiley Imprint
www.josseybass.com

Published by Jossey-Bass
A Wiley Imprint
989 Market Street, San Francisco, CA 94103-1741   www.josseybass.com

Jossey-Bass books and products are available through most bookstores. To contact Jossey-Bass directly call our Customer Care Department within the U.S. at 800-956-7739, outside the U.S. at 317-572-3986 or fax 317-572-4002.

Jossey-Bass also publishes its books in a variety of electronic formats. Some content that appears in print may not be available in electronic books.

Library of Congress Cataloging-in-Publication Data

Abbamont, Gary W.
    Test smart! : ready-to-use test-taking strategies and activities for grades 5–12 /
Gary W. Abbamont, Antoinette Brescher : Illustrated by Cris Guenter.
        p. cm.
    ISBN 0-87628-916-2
    1. Test-taking skills—Handbooks, manuals, etc. 2. Activity programs in
education—Handbooks, manuals, etc. I. Brescher, Antoinette.
LB3060.57.A33 1996
371.26—dc21   96-39568

FIRST EDITION
PB Printing 10 9 8 7 6 5

To Mom and Dad,
who taught, guided, and encouraged me . . .
and
to Katherine, my wife
who will forever inspire me!

—Gary

To Jack, who has always believed in me,
and
To John, who has always made me prove myself.

—Toni

ABOUT THE AUTHORS

Gary W. Abbamont, B.A., Rutgers College, M.A., Columbia University, has taught language arts and social studies for more than twenty years and was named Outstanding Educator in New Jersey. Currently, he is a Principal in the South Brunswick Township School District and has had administrative experience at both the elementary and middle school levels. Gary is an experienced curriculum developer and has assumed responsibility for program implementation in his district.

Antoinette Brescher holds a B.A. degree in elementary education and an M.A. degree in reading from Kean College in New Jersey. She currently teaches science to middle school children at the Gill St. Bernard's School in Gladstone, New Jersey. Mrs. Brescher was the reading consultant writer for the Silver Burdett & Ginn Elementary Science series. She was also recipient of the Edler Hawkins Outstanding Teacher Award.

THE AUTHORS team-taught together while at Crossroads Middle School. They are also the co-authors of *Study Smart! Ready-to-Use Reading / Study Skills Activities for Grades 5-12* (also published by The Center, 1990).

ABOUT THE ARTIST

Cris Guenter, Ed.D., University of Wyoming, Laramie, is currently Professor of Education in fine arts/curriculum and instruction at California State University, Chico. A former K-12 art and gifted and talented teacher in Pennsylvania and Wyoming, Dr. Guenter is also a consultant in arts education and a keynote speaker on the arts in northern California. Her paintings, prints, and photographs have been exhibited in 19 national and international juried exhibitions in the past eight years.

ABOUT THIS BOOK

As a natural outgrowth of learning in our schools, professionals and parents are interested in knowing that students are learning. Such learning is continually evaluated on the basis of teacher-made tests. In addition, standardized testing is a generally accepted assessment tool for measuring achievement and comparing student performance.

Research tells us that strong, effective classroom instruction will result in higher test results in both classroom tests and standardized tests. Research also tells us that helping students learn test-taking strategies will result in increased scores. In this book we intend to help teachers and students become *test smart* through an examination of test-taking strategies and the test-taking requirements often found in the areas of reading, language, and writing. Toward this end, we have developed a series of instructional activities based on the elements found in a wide variety of standardized and teacher-made tests. Throughout the book, a testing tip or strategy is presented followed by one or more activities.

Section 1, *General Test-Taking Strategies,* provides a checklist of strategies designed to teach and reinforce skills in areas such as approaching the test, following test directions, and being aware of test format. This part of the book prepares students for a wide variety of tests they may encounter. Accompanying the checklist are cartoon illustrations suitable for handouts or bulletin board display.

Section 2, *Reading,* focuses its attention on those aspects of reading traditionally found in standardized and classroom tests. Vocabulary is tested in a variety of ways including analogies, synonyms, antonyms, and word parts. Activities are included to increase student confidence when approaching such test items. In addition, students can perform at a higher level in the area of comprehension when the structure of test items is studied in the areas of main idea, sequence, and drawing conclusions.

Section 3, *Language,* presents a variety of activities in which students consider both the form and content of test items in spelling and the conventions of language including proofreading, capitalization, punctuation, and usage.

Section 4, *Writing,* offers activities focusing on the structure of written language. Specifically, students will engage in activities such as the topic sentence, supporting details, sequencing of ideas, sentence structure, and word choice. Since students are frequently called upon to respond in writing to both short-answer and essay-type questions, we have included instructional activities to strengthen students' organization and presentation of such responses.

Each reproducible activity is keyed to the section and states the skill covered, an explanation and example of the skill, a test-taking strategy, and an activity in which the student is able to practice applying the strategy. In some cases, it also includes a follow-up extension activity. This simple format provides a model for you to develop similar activities. You will find that many of the worksheets can be used more than once. For example, the strategy for finding main idea can be used with a limitless number of activities. Repeated use reinforces the skill.

Special features of *Test Smart!* are the reproducible sheets and a complete "Answer Key" for all activities in the book.

Test Smart! provides you with a ready store of activities to teach and reinforce test-taking skills. Its overall aim is to help students understand and develop specific strategies to take tests. With such strategies the student is more likely to approach the test with confidence and demonstrate achievement to the best of his or her ability.

Gary Abbamont
Antoinette Brescher

CONTENTS

Comprehension

Section Three
LANGUAGE
115

Spelling

Mechanics and Usage

Section Four

WRITING
165

Composition

Writing Samples and Open-Ended Responses

ANSWER KEY
209

SECTION ONE

General Test-Taking Strategies

GENERAL TEST-TAKING STRATEGIES

- **Preparing for the Test**
  - — Make and use a study guide.
  - — Listen to the teacher's description of the test and ask questions.
  - — Use your study time well by focusing on the things you don't know.
  - — Study with a friend.
  - — Anticipate the questions you might see on the test.

- **Approaching the Test**
  - — Be prepared.
  - — Study beforehand.
  - — Get a good night's sleep.
  - — Have a healthy breakfast.
  - — Approach the test with a positive attitude.
  - — Use your test results to evaluate what you need to learn.
  - — Think of a test as a way to show what you have learned.

- **Filling Out the Answer Sheet for Standardized Tests**
  - — Listen carefully to directions.
  - — Fill in the answer spaces completely and avoid unnecessary stray marks. Since the tests are often corrected by an automatic scanning machine, filling in the circles completely is very important.
  - — Periodically check the number of the test question with the number on your answer sheet. Be sure they're the same.
  - — Usually your first answer is correct. Only change an answer if you are sure that the change is correct.
  - — Skip those questions you don't know and return to them later. Do not waste time on one question.

- **Filling Out the Answer Sheet for Teacher-Made Tests**
  - — Listen carefully to directions.
  - — Look over the entire test for an overview.
  - — Respond to the question asked.
  - — Focus on key words in the question.
  - — Think before responding.
  - — Narrow your choices.
  - — Read slowly and carefully.
  - — Divide your time according to point values.
  - — Watch for words like *always, never, all,* and *none.* These words usually include or exclude most responses.

— In an essay test, plan before writing.

— Focus on vocabulary.

- **Knowing How Standardized Tests Are Scored**

  — Ask if you will be penalized for unanswered questions. If so, it is better to guess.

  — Keep track of the time allotted to allow you to finish.

  — Go over your answers if there is time.

- **Knowing How Teacher-Made Tests Are Scored**

  — Ask the teacher to explain how points are divided within the test.

  — Divide the time based upon the points awarded in each section. Keep track of the time allotted to allow you to finish.

  — Go over your answers if there is time.

  — Know your teacher's requirements. If vocabulary is stressed in class, use that vocabulary in your responses.

- **Following Directions**

  — Listen and read directions carefully.

  — Watch for signal words such as *first, next, following,* and other sequence words or clues.

  — Focus on verb commands that tell you what to do.

  — Be sure you know what is expected before beginning the test.

- **Testing Format**

  — Ask your teacher about the test format before you start to study.

  — For a fill-in-the-blank test, prepare index cards/flash cards with key words and definitions.

  — For an essay test, use a graphic organizer or web to help you organize information and see relationships.

  — For multiple-choice tests, review your notes and chapter for key words and their definitions.

- **Question Awareness**

  — Become familiar with the types of question patterns often used in tests. Be sure you understand what these patterns require.

- **Narrowing the Odds**

  — In a multiple-choice test, eliminate the answers you know are incorrect. Then make your best guess. If you have only two answers from which to choose, you increase your chances of being successful.

- **Strategies**

  — Learn the many strategies found in this book to help you become a better test taker.

(Test taking is like shooting baskets. If at first you don't succeed, keep with it and try again!)

PREPARING FOR THE TEST !

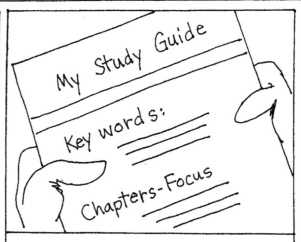

MAKE AND USE A STUDY GUIDE.

LISTEN TO THE TEACHER'S DESCRIPTION OF THE TEST AND ASK QUESTIONS.

USE YOUR STUDY TIME WELL BY FOCUSING ON THINGS YOU DON'T KNOW.

STUDY WITH A FRIEND.

WHAT DID WE DISCUSS? WHAT DID I READ?

WHAT DID THE TEACHER SAY SO MANY TIMES?

WHAT DID MY ASSIGNMENTS COVER? WHAT DO I REMEMBER?

ANTICIPATE THE QUESTIONS YOU MIGHT SEE ON THE TEST.

APPROACHING THE TEST

BE PREPARED.

STUDY BEFOREHAND.

GET A GOOD NIGHT'S SLEEP.

HAVE A HEALTHY BREAKFAST.

APPROACH THE TEST WITH A POSITIVE ATTITUDE.

USE YOUR TEST RESULTS TO EVALUATE WHAT YOU NEED TO LEARN.

THINK OF A TEST AS A WAY TO SHOW WHAT YOU HAVE LEARNED.

FILLING OUT THE ANSWER SHEET FOR STANDARDIZED TESTS

LISTEN CAREFULLY TO DIRECTIONS.

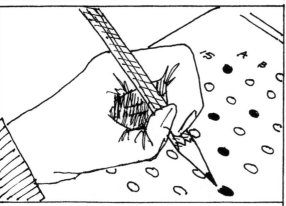

FILL IN THE ANSWER SPACES COMPLETELY AND AVOID UNNECESSARY STRAY MARKS.

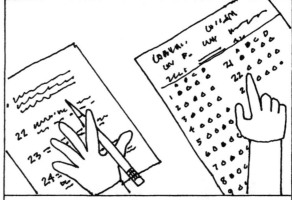

PERIODICALLY CHECK THE NUMBER OF THE TEST QUESTION WITH THE NUMBER ON YOUR ANSWER SHEET.

USUALLY YOUR FIRST ANSWER IS CORRECT. ONLY CHANGE AN ANSWER IF YOU ARE SURE THAT THE CHANGE IS CORRECT.

SKIP THOSE ANSWERS YOU DON'T KNOW AND RETURN TO THEM LATER. DO NOT WASTE TIME ON ONE QUESTION.

FILLING OUT THE ANSWER SHEET FOR TEACHER-MADE TESTS

LISTEN CAREFULLY TO DIRECTIONS.

LOOK OVER THE ENTIRE TEST FOR AN OVERVIEW.

RESPOND TO THE QUESTION ASKED.

FOCUS ON KEY WORDS IN THE QUESTION.

THINK BEFORE RESPONDING.

NARROW YOUR CHOICES.

READ SLOWLY AND CAREFULLY.

DIVIDE YOUR TIME ACCORDING TO POINT VALUES.

WATCH FOR WORDS LIKE *ALWAYS, NEVER, ALL* AND *NONE*. THESE WORDS USUALLY INCLUDE OR EXCLUDE MOST RESPONSES.

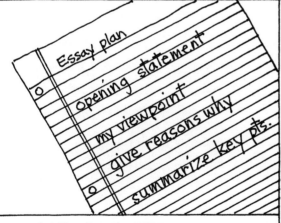

IN AN ESSAY TEST, PLAN BEFORE WRITING.

Describe...
    Analyze...
        INTERPRET...
    List... compare...

FOCUS ON VOCABULARY.

KNOWING HOW STANDARDIZED TESTS ARE SCORED

ASK IF YOU WILL BE PENALIZED FOR UNANSWERED QUESTIONS. IF SO, IT IS BETTER TO GUESS.

KEEP TRACK OF THE TIME ALLOTTED TO ALLOW YOU TO FINISH.

GO OVER YOUR ANSWERS IF THERE IS TIME.

KNOWING HOW TEACHER-MADE TESTS ARE SCORED

ASK THE TEACHER TO EXPLAIN HOW POINTS ARE DIVIDED WITHIN THE TEST.

DIVIDE THE TIME BASED UPON THE POINTS AWARDED IN EACH SECTION. KEEP TRACK OF THE TIME ALLOTTED TO ALLOW YOU TO FINISH.

GO OVER YOUR ANSWERS IF THERE IS TIME.

KNOW YOUR TEACHER'S REQUIREMENTS. IF VOCABULARY IS STRESSED IN CLASS, USE THAT VOCABULARY IN YOUR RESPONSES.

FOLLOWING DIRECTIONS

LISTEN AND READ DIRECTIONS CAREFULLY.

First NEXT

FOLLOWING

After before

WATCH FOR SIGNAL WORDS SUCH AS FIRST, NEXT, FOLLOWING AND OTHER SEQUENCE WORDS OR CLUES.

Compare the two points of view.

Match the word to the definition.

Illustrate and label the parts of a cell.

FOCUS ON VERB COMMANDS WHICH TELL YOU WHAT TO DO.

ANY QUESTIONS BEFORE WE BEGIN?

BE SURE YOU KNOW WHAT IS EXPECTED BEFORE BEGINNING THE TEST.

TESTING FORMAT

ASK YOUR TEACHER ABOUT THE TEST FORMAT BEFORE YOU START TO STUDY.

FOR A FILL-IN-THE-BLANK TEST, PREPARE INDEX/FLASH CARDS WITH KEY WORDS AND DEFINITIONS.

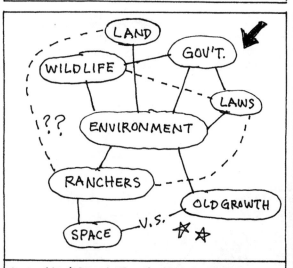

FOR AN ESSAY TEST, USE A GRAPHIC ORGANIZER OR WEB TO HELP YOU ORGANIZE INFORMATION AND SEE RELATIONSHIPS.

FOR MULTIPLE-CHOICE TESTS, REVIEW YOUR NOTES AND CHAPTER FOR KEY WORDS AND THEIR DEFINITIONS.

QUESTION AWARENESS

BECOME FAMILIAR WITH THE TYPES OF QUESTION PATTERNS OFTEN USED IN TESTS. BE SURE YOU UNDERSTAND WHAT THESE PATTERNS REQUIRE.

NARROWING THE ODDS

IN A MULTIPLE-CHOICE TEST, ELIMINATE THE ANSWERS THAT YOU KNOW ARE INCORRECT. THEN MAKE YOUR BEST GUESS. IF YOU HAVE ONLY TWO ANSWERS FROM WHICH TO CHOOSE, YOU INCREASE YOUR CHANCES OF BEING SUCCESSFUL.

STRATEGIES

LEARN THE MANY STRATEGIES FOUND IN THIS BOOK TO HELP YOU BECOME A BETTER TEST TAKER.

SECTION TWO

Reading

VOCABULARY

COMPREHENSION

VOCABULARY

Standardized and classroom tests often use similar vocabulary when presenting test questions and directions. Familiarity with these words and phrasings can be helpful when taking such tests. Increased understanding of these words and phrases will help you in responding to such test questions.

Here are some common directions used on standardized tests:

- Read the sentence and choose the meaning of the underlined word.

- Choose the best synonym for the underlined word in the sentence.

- Choose the word that best completes the sentence.

- Choose the word or group of words that means the same, or about the same, as the underlined word.

- Read the two sentences. Then choose the word that best completes both sentences.

- Read the sentence and answer the question.

- In which sentence is the word _____ used incorrectly.

- Choose the word(s) that most precisely fit the meaning of the sentence.

- The word _____ in line _____ is best interpreted to mean:

- Choose the word(s) that, when inserted in the sentence, best fit(s) the meaning of the sentence as a whole.

- Which of the following word best fits into the list above?

- Which of the following best replaces the word _____ in the passage?

- Fill in the blank with the word that most precisely fits the context of the sentence.

2-1. A STRATEGY FOR RECOGNIZING ANALOGIES

Analogies are pairs of words related in some way. Given a set of words, you are challenged to determine how they are related and to apply this relationship to a second set of words.

Example: hammer : nail as bat : _____

     A. glove
     B. ball
     C. home plate
     D. baseball cap

Relationship: Just as a *hammer* is an implement used to strike a *nail* and power it in a forward direction, so must the bat be related to the correct answer. In this case, the *bat* is an implement used to hit a *ball* and power it forward. The remaining choices do not fit this pattern.

TESTING TIP:

When faced with an analogy question, put the first two words into a single sentence that explains their relationship. Then substitute the first word of the second pair into the same sentence with each of the choices to determine the best answer.

Sample: cactus : desert as kelp : _____
     A. seaweed
     B. rain forest
     C. tundra
     D. ocean

Relationship Sentence: A cactus is a plant growing in the desert as kelp is a plant growing in the _____.

Explanation: Look at the illustration of this analogy on the next page to help you see the relationship. Try using each one of the four choices in the blank in order to determine the best answer. Seaweed is not correct because kelp does not grow in seaweed. Rain forest is not correct because kelp does not grow in the rain forest. Tundra is not correct because kelp does not grow in the tundra. Ocean is the correct choice since kelp is a type of seaweed that grows in the ocean.

CACTUS / DESERT SCENE

KELP /

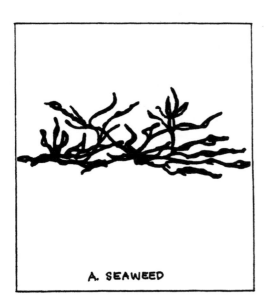

A. SEAWEED

B. RAINFOREST

C. TUNDRA

D. OCEAN

Name_____ Date_____

2-1A. RECOGNIZING ANALOGIES

Activity: Choose the word that best completes each analogy and circle the correct letter. Then write a sentence to best explain the relationship between each pair of words presented.

1. moon : night as sun : _____
   A. fun
   B. day
   C. light
   D. lunch

   _____

   _____

2. engine : car as heart : _____
   A. lungs
   B. love
   C. body
   D. mind

   _____

   _____

3. calf : cow as colt : _____
   A. deer
   B. gun
   C. mare
   D. stallion

   _____

   _____

4. pencil : paper as mouse : _____
   A. trap
   B. cat
   C. computer
   D. cheese

   _____

   _____

5. ticket : admission as key : _____
   A. knowledge
   B. lock
   C. door
   D. entrance

   _____

   _____

2-1A. Continued

6. touchdown : football as goal : _____
   A. soccer
   B. basketball
   C. golf
   D. swimming

   _____

   _____

7. winter : snow as summer : _____
   A. travel
   B. rain
   C. heat
   D. surf

   _____

   _____

8. coach : tennis as teacher : _____
   A. history
   B. book
   C. student
   D. classroom

   _____

   _____

9. rise : sink as forward : _____
   A. upward
   B. sideward
   C. shift
   D. backward

   _____

   _____

10. kitchen : house as classroom : _____
    A. hallway
    B. town
    C. school
    D. community

    _____

    _____

Extension: Generate five original pairs of analogies as shown above and develop a sentence to explain the relationship for each.

Name_____ Date_____

2-1B. RECOGNIZING ANALOGIES

Activity: Choose the word that best completes each analogy and circle the correct letter. Then identify the relationship and write a sentence to best explain the relationship between each pair of words presented.

1. ounce : pound as inch : _____
   A. liter
   B. ton
   C. meter
   D. foot

   _____

   _____

2. chick : hen as fawn : _____
   A. buck
   B. doe
   C. deer
   D. stag

   _____

   _____

3. puddle : lake as hill : _____
   A. mud
   B. valley
   C. mountain
   D. stream

   _____

   _____

4. basement : penthouse as roots : _____
   A. tree
   B. trunk
   C. leaves
   D. bark

   _____

   _____

5. petal : flower as page : _____
   A. classroom
   B. book
   C. school
   D. speaker

   _____

   _____

2-1B. Continued

6. snow : skiers as waves : _____
   A. boat
   B. wind
   C. surfers
   D. toboggan

   _____

   _____

7. class : students as army : _____
   A. soldiers
   B. tanks
   C. uniforms
   D. school

   _____

   _____

8. city : county as state : _____
   A. town
   B. province
   C. American
   D. country

   _____

   _____

9. ice cream : sundae as pasta : _____
   A. lasagna
   B. meatballs
   C. pizza
   D. Italian

   _____

   _____

10. shoelace : sneakers as zipper : _____
    A. belt
    B. jacket
    C. t-shirt
    D. sock

    _____

    _____

2-2. A STRATEGY FOR RECOGNIZING RELATIONSHIPS IN ANALOGIES

Analogies are pairs of words related in some way. Given a set of words, you are challenged to determine how they are related and to apply this relationship to a second set of words. While there is a wide range of possible relationships, there are some that are often used.

Analogy Example	*Relationship*
toe : foot as finger : hand	part / whole
joey : kangaroo as cub : lion	young / adult
golf ball : basketball as mouse : elephant	small / large
canyon : ditch as ocean : river	large / small
funny : hysterical as whisper : shout	degree
rain : mud as sunset : darkness	cause / effect
ceiling : floor as sky : ground	above / below

TESTING TIP:

When faced with an analogy question, identify the relationship that exists in the first pair. Use this relationship to help guide you to the correct answer. Put the first two words into a single sentence that explains their relationship. Then substitute the first word of the second pair into the same sentence with each of the choices to determine the best answer.

Sample: word : sentence as page : _____
                   A.   theater
                   B.   paragraph
                   C.   book
                   D.   library

Relationship Sentence: A word is a part of a sentence as a page is part of a _____.

Explanation: Look at the illustration of this analogy on the next page to help you see the relationship. Try using each one of the four choices in the blank in order to determine the best answer. Theater is not correct since a page is not a part of it. Paragraph is also not correct since a page is not part of a paragraph. A page is not part of a library, but a page *is* part of a book.

The wagon train set up 〔CAMP〕 along the bend in the river.

HIGHLIGHTED WORD/SENTENCE

PAGE FROM BOOK

A. THEATER

B. PARAGRAPH

C. BOOK

D. LIBRARY

Name_____ Date_____

2-2A. RECOGNIZING RELATIONSHIPS IN ANALOGIES

Activity: Choose the word that best completes each analogy and circle the correct letter. Then state the relationship and write a sentence to best explain the relationship between each pair of words presented.

1. pebble : boulder as puddle : _____
   A. mud
   B. splash
   C. ocean
   D. rain
   Relationship: _____
   Sentence: _____
   _____

2. stroll : run as tap : _____
   A. annoy
   B. tickle
   C. murmur
   D. clobber
   Relationship: _____
   Sentence: _____
   _____

3. chandelier : table as balcony : _____
   A. orchestra
   B. theater
   C. actors
   D. intermission
   Relationship: _____
   Sentence: _____
   _____

4. virus : disease as mosquito : _____
   A. itching
   B. larva
   C. buzzing
   D. lotion
   Relationship: _____
   Sentence: _____
   _____

5. tadpole : frog as puppy : _____
   A. dog
   B. kitten
   C. owner
   D. housebroken
   Relationship: _____
   Sentence: _____
   _____

2-2A. Continued

6. city : village as mansion : _____
   A. cottage
   B. kitchen
   C. apartment
   D. skyscraper
   Relationship: _____
   Sentence: _____
   _____

7. pie : slice as orange : _____
   A. peel
   B. wedge
   C. fruit
   D. apple
   Relationship: _____
   Sentence: _____
   _____

8. evaporation : clouds as condensation : _____
   A. drops
   B. ice
   C. sun
   D. wind
   Relationship: _____
   Sentence: _____
   _____

9. lime : hunter as pink : _____
   A. fisherman
   B. hot
   C. cranberry
   D. yellow
   Relationship: _____
   Sentence: _____
   _____

10. sunken ship : water as buried treasure : _____
    A. chest
    B. pirate
    C. sand
    D. ship
    Relationship: _____
    Sentence: _____
    _____

2-3. ANOTHER STRATEGY FOR RECOGNIZING RELATIONSHIPS IN ANALOGIES

Analogies are pairs of words related in some way. Given a set of words, you are challenged to determine how they are related and to apply this relationship to a second set of words. While there is a wide range of possible relationships, there are some that are often used.

Analogy Example	*Relationship*
saturated : parched as ornate : plain	antonyms
lengthy : extensive as hot : torrid	synonyms
blade : cut as hatchet : chop	tool / function
peas : pod as peanuts : shell	inside / outside
crustacean : lobster as mammal : whale	category / member
cookies : baker as sculpture : artist	product / producer
merchant : store as pilot : cockpit	person / location
quarterback : passing as lawyer : defending	person / action

TESTING TIP:

When faced with an analogy question, identify the relationship that exists in the first pair. Use this relationship to help guide you to the correct answer. Once again, put the first two words into a single sentence that explains their relationship. Then substitute the first word of the second pair into the same sentence with each of the choices to determine the best answer.

Sample: hammer : tool as chair : _____
      A.   legs
      B.   comfortable
      C.   cushion
      D.   furniture

Relationship Sentence: A hammer is a member of the tool category as a chair is a member of the _____ category.

Explanation: Look at the illustration of this analogy on the next page to help you see the relationship. Try using each one of the four choices in the blank in order to determine the best answer. Legs is not a category to which the chair belongs. Comfortable is also not a category to which the chair belongs. The chair is not a member of the cushion category; however, the chair does belong to the category of furniture.

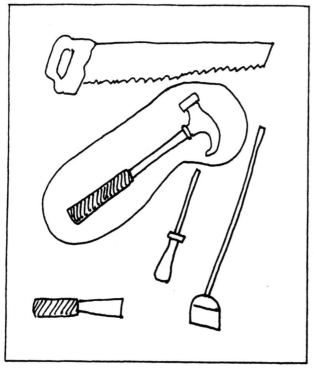

HAMMER / GROUP OF TOOLS

CHAIR

A. CHAIR LEGS

B. COMFORTABLE

C. CUSHION

D. FURNITURE

Name_____ Date_____

2-3A. RECOGNIZING RELATIONSHIPS IN ANALOGIES

Activity: Read the first pair of words in each analogy and identify the relationship. Then think of a word to complete the analogy. Finally, write a sentence to explain the relationship and check to see that your word makes sense.

1. ruler : measure as toothbrush : _____

   Relationship: _____

   Sentence: _____

   _____

2. passenger : automobile as resident : _____

   Relationship: _____

   Sentence: _____

   _____

3. warden : prison as teller : _____

   Relationship: _____

   Sentence: _____

   _____

4. glossy : dull as wealthy : _____

   Relationship: _____

   Sentence: _____

   _____

5. police officer : protect as doctor : _____

   Relationship: _____

   Sentence: _____

   _____

6. director : film as author : _____

   Relationship: _____

   Sentence: _____

   _____

2-3A. Continued

7. beverage : drink as forest : _____

   Relationship: _____

   Sentence: _____

   _____

8. colonial : house as trout : _____

   Relationship: _____

   Sentence: _____

   _____

9. teacher : instructs as mechanic : _____

   Relationship: _____

   Sentence: _____

   _____

10. fluid : container as letter : _____

   Relationship: _____

   Sentence: _____

   _____

Extension: Generate five original pairs of analogies as shown above, identify the relationship for each, and write an original sentence proving the relationship.

2-4. A STRATEGY FOR RECOGNIZING SYNONYMS

Synonyms are two words that share the same meaning. Given a word, you are challenged to search a series of words in an effort to determine the one word that is the same in meaning.

Word	*Synonym*	*Explanation*
difficult	challenging	*Difficult* means hard or challenging. *Challenging* is a **synonym** for *difficult* since both share the same meaning.

TESTING TIP:

Most reading sections of the standard achievement tests include a subtest in vocabulary. Within the vocabulary section, there are usually some test items involving synonyms, words with the same meanings. Sometimes the words are presented in isolation; sometimes the words are presented to the test taker in context.

Sample: Which of the following words has the SAME meaning as the word ***ordinary***?
   A.   special
   B.   plain
   C.   tough
   D.   unusual

Explanation: Since ***plain*** and ***ordinary*** share the same meaning, ***plain*** is the correct answer choice here.

2-4A. RECOGNIZING SYNONYMS

Activity: Below is a sample of synonyms presented in isolation. In this situation use the word in a sentence. Then replace the word with each of the four choices. Also, use the process of elimination to narrow the list of reasonable choices.

1. Which of the following words is the SYNONYM for the word *night*?
   A. evening
   B. afternoon
   C. dawn
   D. ghosts

Write a sentence below using the boldfaced word. Then replace the word with each of the above choices to see which makes the most sense.

_____

_____

2. Which of the following words is the SYNONYM for the word *increase*?
   A. large
   B. add
   C. lessen
   D. subtract

Write a sentence below using the boldfaced word. Then replace the word with each of the above choices to see which makes the most sense.

_____

_____

3. Which of the following words is the SYNONYM for the word *find*?
   A. missing
   B. lose
   C. treasure
   D. locate

Write a sentence below using the boldfaced word. Then replace the word with each of the above choices to see which makes the most sense.

_____

_____

2-4A. Continued

4. Which of the following words is the SYNONYM for the word *old*?
   A. ancient
   B. history
   C. recent
   D. wrinkled

Write a sentence below using the boldfaced word. Then replace the word with each of the above choices to see which makes the most sense.

_____

_____

5. Which of the following words is the SYNONYM for the word *walk*?
   A. gallop
   B. skip
   C. canter
   D. stroll

Write a sentence below using the boldfaced word. Then replace the word with each of the above choices to see which makes the most sense.

_____

_____

6. Which of the following words is the SYNONYM for the word *picture*?
   A. color
   B. draw
   C. beautiful
   D. photo

Write a sentence below using the boldfaced word. Then replace the word with each of the above choices to see which makes the most sense.

_____

_____

7. Which of the following words is the SYNONYM for the word *open*?
   A. doorway
   B. exit
   C. unlock
   D. pathway

Write a sentence below using the boldfaced word. Then replace the word with each of the above choices to see which makes the most sense.

_____

_____

2-4A. Continued

8. Which of the following words is the SYNONYM for the word *road*?
   A. sidewalk
   B. driveway
   C. trail
   D. street

   Write a sentence below using the boldfaced word. Then replace the word with each of the above choices to see which makes the most sense.

   _____

   _____

9. Which of the following words is the SYNONYM for the word *important*?
   A. optional
   B. necessary
   C. acceptable
   D. helpful

   Write a sentence below using the boldfaced word. Then replace the word with each of the above choices to see which makes the most sense.

   _____

   _____

10. Which of the following words is the SYNONYM for the word *below*?
    A. floor
    B. basement
    C. feet
    D. underneath

    Write a sentence below using the boldfaced word. Then replace the word with each of the above choices to see which makes the most sense.

    _____

    _____

Extension: Generate five original synonym test items as shown above, generate the original sentences, indicate the correct choice, and explain how the words are similar.

2-4B. RECOGNIZING SYNONYMS

Activity: Below is a sample of synonyms presented in isolation. In this situation use the word in a sentence. Then replace the word with each of the four choices. Also, use the process of elimination to narrow the list of reasonable choices.

1. Which of the following words is a SYNONYM for the word ***obstruct***?

    A. block

    B. observe

    C. burglar

    D. vague

Write a sentence below using the boldfaced word. Then replace the word with each of the above choices to see which makes the most sense.

_____

_____

2. Which of the following words is a SYNONYM for the word ***significant***?

    A. worthless

    B. gesture

    C. meaningful

    D. omen

Write a sentence below using the boldfaced word. Then replace the word with each of the above choices to see which makes the most sense.

_____

_____

3. Which of the following words is a SYNONYM for the word ***flamboyant***?

    A. showy

    B. understated

    C. flammable

    D. fierce

Write a sentence below using the boldfaced word. Then replace the word with each of the above choices to see which makes the most sense.

_____

_____

2-4B. Continued

4. Which of the following words is a SYNONYM for the word *concern*?
   - A. interest
   - B. confirm
   - C. appropriate
   - D. confident

   Write a sentence below using the boldfaced word. Then replace the word with each of the above choices to see which makes the most sense.

   _____

   _____

5. Which of the following words is a SYNONYM for the word *liberty*?
   - A. justice
   - B. equality
   - C. prejudice
   - D. freedom

   Write a sentence below using the boldfaced word. Then replace the word with each of the above choices to see which makes the most sense.

   _____

   _____

6. Which of the following words is a SYNONYM for the word *genuine*?
   - A. imitation
   - B. authentic
   - C. hereditary
   - D. generous

   Write a sentence below using the boldfaced word. Then replace the word with each of the above choices to see which makes the most sense.

   _____

   _____

7. Which of the following words is a SYNONYM for the word *reject*?
   - A. accept
   - B. regret
   - C. refuse
   - D. eject

   Write a sentence below using the boldfaced word. Then replace the word with each of the above choices to see which makes the most sense.

   _____

   _____

2-4A. Continued

8. Which of the following words is a SYNONYM for the word ***volunteer***?
   A. offer
   B. victorious
   C. shelter
   D. resign

   Write a sentence below using the boldfaced word. Then replace the word with each of the above choices to see which makes the most sense.

   _____

   _____

9. Which of the following words is a SYNONYM for the word ***aggravate***?
   A. fabricate
   B. consult
   C. adhesive
   D. irritate

   Write a sentence below using the boldfaced word. Then replace the word with each of the above choices to see which makes the most sense.

   _____

   _____

10. Which of the following words is a SYNONYM for the word ***distinct***?
    A. distant
    B. obscure
    C. clear
    D. distract

    Write a sentence below using the boldfaced word. Then replace the word with each of the above choices to see which makes the most sense.

    _____

    _____

2-5. ANOTHER STRATEGY FOR RECOGNIZING SYNONYMS

Synonyms are two words that share the same meaning. Given a word, you are challenged to search a series of words in an effort to determine the one word that is the same in meaning.

Word	Synonym	Explanation
difficult	challenging	*Difficult* means hard or challenging. *Challenging* is a **synonym** for *difficult* since both share the same meaning.

TESTING TIP:

Most reading sections of the standard achievement tests include a subtest in vocabulary. Within the vocabulary section, there are usually some test items involving synonyms, words with the same meanings. Sometimes the words are presented in isolation; sometimes the words are presented to the test taker in context.

Sample: Her birthday cake was quite ordinary as it had little color and design. Which of the following words has the SAME meaning as the word ***ordinary***?

    A. special
    B. plain
    C. tough
    D. unusual

Explanation: Since ***plain*** and ***ordinary*** share the same meaning, ***plain*** is the correct answer choice here.

Name_____ **Date**_____

2-5A. RECOGNIZING SYNONYMS

Activity: Read each of the following sentences and its four word choices. Then replace the boldfaced word in the sentence with each of the four choices. Finally, select the word that is closest in meaning to the boldfaced word.

1. While Anthony worked at his station on the automobile assembly line, doing the same task over and over again became **tedious**.
    A. exciting
    B. boring
    C. educational
    D. stimulating

2. The **emerald** skirt matched the shade of rainforest plants.
    A. rose
    B. green
    C. purple
    D. tailored

3. Last summer our family **started** a new tradition.
    A. initiated
    B. ended
    C. followed
    D. found

4. Camp Hiahleah was the source of many fine childhood **friends**, many of whom I still see today.
    A. companions
    B. memories
    C. workers
    D. counselors

5. Raise your hand when you have an **answer** to the math problem.
    A. response
    B. contribution
    C. talking
    D. question

6. Everyone can use **help** when moving a piece of heavy furniture.
    A. hand
    B. money
    C. polite
    D. assistance

2-5A. Continued

7. At exactly twelve noon the trumpets **sounded**.
   A. listened
   B. silenced
   C. blared
   D. shined

8. The children had a **difficult** choice to make because they all loved both pizza and hot dogs.
   A. big
   B. easy
   C. troublesome
   D. simple

9. Several hours had passed before it was time to **go** from Gate 64 to our plane.
   A. depart
   B. enter
   C. visit
   D. arrive

10. For our spring vacation, we took a cruise out of the bay into the **ocean**.
    A. river
    B. sea
    C. salty
    D. water

2-6. A STRATEGY FOR RECOGNIZING ANTONYMS

Antonyms are two words that are opposite in meaning. Given a word, you are challenged to search a series of words in an effort to determine the one word that is opposite in meaning.

Word	*Antonym*	*Explanation*
difficult	easy	*Difficult* means hard or challenging whereas *easy* means accomplished without much effort. The **opposite** of *difficult* is *easy*. *Easy* is called an **antonym** of *difficult*.

TESTING TIP:

Most reading sections of the standard achievement tests include a subtest in vocabulary. Within the vocabulary section, there are usually some test items involving antonyms, words with opposite meanings. Sometimes the words are presented in isolation; sometimes the words are presented to the test taker in context. Below is a sample of antonyms presented in isolation. In this situation you should use the process of elimination to help you determine the correct answer. Be careful not to select a word with the same meaning. Students often forget that they are looking for opposites, not synonyms.

Sample: Which of the following words is the ANTONYM for the word **ordinary**?
  A. special
  B. plain
  C. tough
  D. regular

Explanation: Use the word in a sentence. Then replace the word with each of the four choices. Also, use the process of elimination to narrow the list of reasonable choices. *Plain* and *regular* are synonyms for *ordinary*. *Tough* means difficult and does not relate to the word *ordinary*. The correct choice is *special* because it is the opposite of *ordinary*.

45

2-6A. RECOGNIZING ANTONYMS

Activity: Select the word most opposite in meaning to the boldfaced word. Then write a sentence explaining your choice.

1. Which of the following words is the ANTONYM for the word *deep*?
   A. dark
   B. intense
   C. far
   D. shallow

   _____

   _____

2. Which of the following words is the ANTONYM for the word *delicate*?
   A. fragile
   B. fine
   C. sturdy
   D. breakable

   _____

   _____

3. Which of the following words is the ANTONYM for the word *famous*?
   A. shy
   B. popular
   C. unknown
   D. recognizable

   _____

   _____

4. Which of the following words is the ANTONYM for the word *complicated*?
   A. simple
   B. detailed
   C. tough
   D. confusing

   _____

   _____

5. Which of the following words is the ANTONYM for the word *warlike*?
   A. vengeful
   B. peaceful
   C. aggressive
   D. military

   _____

   _____

2-6A. Continued

6. Which of the following words is the ANTONYM for the word *modern*?
    A. contemporary
    B. updated
    C. new
    D. old-fashioned

    _____

    _____

7. Which of the following words is the ANTONYM for the word *steep*?
    A. high
    B. level
    C. inclined
    D. mountainous

    _____

    _____

8. Which of the following words is the ANTONYM for the word *challenging*?
    A. demanding
    B. easy
    C. tough
    D. regular

    _____

    _____

9. Which of the following words is the ANTONYM for the word *slow*?
    A. brisk
    B. lethargic
    C. immobile
    D. steady

    _____

    _____

10. Which of the following words is the ANTONYM for the word *expensive*?
    A. over-priced
    B. cheap
    C. reasonable
    D. outrageous

    _____

    _____

Extension: Generate five original antonym test items as shown above, generate the original sentences, indicate the correct choice, and explain how the words are opposite.

2-7. ANOTHER STRATEGY FOR RECOGNIZING ANTONYMS

Antonyms are two words that are opposite in meaning. Given a word, you are challenged to search a series of words in an effort to determine the one word that is opposite in meaning.

Word	Antonym	Explanation
difficult	easy	*Difficult* means hard or challenging whereas *easy* means accomplished without much effort. The **opposite** of *difficult* is *easy*. *Easy* is called an **antonym** of *difficult*.

TESTING TIP:

Most reading sections of the standard achievement tests include a subtest in vocabulary. Within the vocabulary section, there are usually some test items involving antonyms, words with opposite meanings. Sometimes the words are presented in isolation; sometimes the words are presented to the test taker in context. Below is a sample of antonyms presented in context. In this situation you should use the context of the passage to help you determine the correct answer. Use each of the four possible answers to replace the given word to see which one is most opposite in meaning.

Sample: The woman stood with **pride,** her hand placed firmly on her chest, as she sang the national anthem.

A. confidence
B. pleasure
C. loyalty
D. shame

Explanation: Replace the boldfaced word in the sentence with each of the four possibilities to determine the word that is most opposite in meaning. Also, use the process of elimination to narrow the list of reasonable choices. Use the context clues to help you select your choice. In this case the word **shame** is most opposite of **pride.**

2-7A. RECOGNIZING ANTONYMS

Activity: Below is a series of sentences each containing a boldfaced word. Your task is to find the antonym for each of these words and circle your letter choice. Try substituting each of the choices in the sentence in order to find the word most opposite in meaning of the boldfaced word.

1. The pattern of the patchwork quilt was **intricate** and must have taken much patience and skill to create. Which of the following words is the ANTONYM for the word **intricate**?
   A. complicated
   B. sophisticated
   C. plain
   D. colorful

2. Their dance moves on the floor were **quick** and polished and appreciated by the audience. Which of the following words is the ANTONYM for the word **quick**?
   A. brisk
   B. sharp
   C. fast
   D. slow

3. Today's newspaper contains an article about the recent snowstorms and the **challenges** they present us. Which of the following words is the ANTONYM for the word **challenges**?
   A. obstacles
   B. opportunities
   C. problems
   D. difficulties

4. The **brilliant** inventor stunned the world with the new medicine. Which of the following words is the ANTONYM for the word **brilliant**?
   A. intelligent
   B. talented
   C. average
   D. gifted

5. With only ten days left until we **went** home, my friend finally wrote a letter to his parents. Which of the following words is the ANTONYM for the word **went**?
   A. traveled
   B. journeyed
   C. stayed
   D. drove

2-7A. Continued

6. Today's computers can create pictures of **amazing** detail. Which of the following words is the ANTONYM for the word **amazing**?

   A. wonderful

   B. ordinary

   C. incredible

   D. striking

7. For three hours the singer **entertained** the audience. Which of the following words is the ANTONYM for the word **entertained**?

   A. bored

   B. engaged

   C. treated

   D. stimulated

8. Several members of the circus family **traveled** for months at a time. Which of the following words is the ANTONYM for the word **traveled**?

   A. journeyed

   B. remained

   C. drove

   D. moved

9. If it wasn't for the **slow** hare, the turtle would never have won the race. Which of the following words is the ANTONYM for the word **slow**?

   A. quick

   B. lethargic

   C. immobile

   D. sluggish

10. **Mannerly** children are usually invited to many parties. Which of the following words is the ANTONYM for the word **mannerly**?

    A. polite

    B. well-behaved

    C. rude

    D. respectful

2-8. A STRATEGY FOR DETERMINING VOCABULARY IN CONTEXT

Vocabulary in context is tested in a sentence or short passage. The passage is presented with a blank or pair of blanks where the vocabulary belongs. You are asked to determine which word or pair of words best fit into the passage.

Example: Having a vocabulary typical of an adult, the young child was described as _____.

    A. fickle
    B. precocious
    C. arrogant
    D. frugal

Explanation: The sentence indicates that the missing word will compare the child with an adult in terms of his or her vocabulary.

    A. *Fickle* means changeable, unsteady.
    B. *Precocious* means bright at an early age.
    C. *Arrogant* means overly proud.
    D. *Frugal* means thrifty.

Precocious is the correct answer.

TESTING TIP:

Read the sentence to find clues that will help you determine meaning in the sentence. See if you can use other words in the sentence to fill in the blank before looking at the list of choices. Then read the list for a synonym for that word. Be sure that the word you select fits grammatically within the sentence. For example, if the sentence needs a noun, do not select a verb form.

2-8A. DETERMINING VOCABULARY IN CONTEXT

Activity: Use the testing tip in order to find the best word for each sentence.

1. He never read his homework assignments. Therefore, he failed all his daily quizzes and learned to _____ ancient history.
   A. reprimand
   B. deplore
   C. enhance
   D. appreciate

2. Through studying the leaf identification chart, Jennifer learned to _____ poison ivy from Virginia creeper.
   A. differentiate
   B. discrepancy
   C. recognize
   D. produce

3. The teacher _____ the class for trading names to confuse the substitute teacher.
   A. reprimand
   B. acclaimed
   C. admonished
   D. paroled

4. When Angelica reviewed Paolo's written composition, she offered him some _____ suggestions that helped him improve his paper.
   A. ineffectual
   B. constructive
   C. mediocre
   D. destructive

5. Because of her _____ attitude, the new girl had difficulty making friends.
   A. amiable
   B. sympathetic
   C. belligerent
   D. affable

6. Since the issue was so _____, the citizens at the town meeting became enraged as they argued both sides.
   A. passive
   B. mundane
   C. persistent
   D. controversial

2-8A. *Continued*

7. The doctor's prescription helped to _____ the patient's severe itching, and therefore, enabled him to get a good night's sleep.

    A. worsen

    B. alleviate

    C. foster

    D. perpetuate

8. Because of the child's fear of ghosts, he was _____ to enter the haunted house on Halloween.

    A. enthusiastic

    B. fearless

    C. zealous

    D. reluctant

9. She showed her _____ through working at the video game until she attained a score surpassing that of her friend.

    A. persistence

    B. resignation

    C. persevere

    D. intelligence

10. When confronted with a problem, a _____ person can come up with alternative solutions.

    A. respectable

    B. narrow-minded

    C. resourceful

    D. reticent

Extension: Create five original sentences like those above and provide four possible answers. Indicate your correct choice and explain why it is correct.

2-9. ANOTHER STRATEGY FOR DETERMINING VOCABULARY IN CONTEXT (CHALLENGE LEVEL)

Vocabulary in context is tested in a sentence or short passage. The passage is presented with a blank or pair of blanks where the vocabulary belongs. You are asked to determine which word or pair of words best fits into the passage.

Example: Having a vocabulary typical of an adult, the young child was described as _____.

    A. fickle
    B. precocious
    C. arrogant
    D. frugal

Explanation: The sentence indicates that the missing word will compare the child with an adult in terms of his or her vocabulary.

    A. *Fickle* means changeable, unsteady.
    B. *Precocious* means bright at an early age.
    C. *Arrogant* means overly proud.
    D. *Frugal* means thrifty.

    Precocious is the correct answer.

TESTING TIP:

Read the sentence to find clues that will help you determine meaning in the sentence. See if you can use other words in the sentence to fill in the blank before looking at the list of choices. Then read the list for a synonym for that word. Be sure that the word you select fits grammatically within the sentence. For example, if the sentence needs a noun, do not select a verb form.

Name_____ Date_____

2-9A. DETERMINING VOCABULARY IN CONTEXT
(CHALLENGE LEVEL)

Activity: Use the testing tip in order to find the best word for each sentence.

1. His decision to take the late night flight from Los Angeles to New York was a good one. It allowed him to make an important early morning meeting and further _____ a successful product line that his company manufactured.
   A. rescind
   B. sponsor
   C. enhance
   D. speculate

2. As a result of the salesperson's angry tone, the child _____ in the corner and refused to talk to even his own mother.
   A. reprimanded
   B. dispelled
   C. cowered
   D. countered

3. The woman was so _____ by the far-out answer that she asked her friend the question a second time.
   A. illuminated
   B. baffled
   C. embracing
   D. assured

4. In addition to the candidate's fine public relations work, he also dressed _____.
   A. tawdry
   B. routinely
   C. impeccably
   D. sultry

5. Because of her positive attitude, the woman had _____ many disbelievers to her cause.
   A. extended
   B. rallied
   C. resumed
   D. dissuaded

6. Efforts to rebuild the fallen candidate's campaign met with pure disaster, so she decided to _____ efforts to renew her campaign.
   A. forsake
   B. fortify
   C. launch
   D. propel

2-9A. Continued

7. The doctor's prescription helped to _____ the patient's worsening condition, and so the patient was most grateful for the medicine.
   A. exacerbate
   B. mitigate
   C. hamper
   D. perpetuate

8. The students' low grades on the recent test prompted the teacher to _____ his teaching strategies.
   A. embrace
   B. reconsider
   C. absolve
   D. champion

9. The child showed his _____ when refusing to give in to the older children's success with the video games.
   A. resourcefulness
   B. resignation
   C. perseverence
   D. exemplary

10. When confronted with a new situation, a(n) _____ person is likely to come up with successful alternative solutions.
    A. rigid
    B. reasonless
    C. inflexible
    D. resilient

Extension: Create five original sentences like those above and provide four possible answers. Indicate your correct choice and explain why it is correct.

2-10. A THIRD STRATEGY FOR VOCABULARY IN CONTEXT

Vocabulary is often tested within the context of a sentence or short passage. The passage is presented with a blank or pair of blanks where the vocabulary belongs. You are asked to determine which word or pair best fits into the passage.

Example: His _____ research on the subject of the rain forest _____ him to convince the government to protect the rare plant.

    A.   limited – forced
    B.   scholarly – prevented
    C.   extensive – enabled
    D.   elementary – fostered

Explanation: In this sentence an adjective to describe research and a verb to complete the sentence are needed. The sentence further explains that he was successful in convincing the government.

    A.   *Limited* research would not be convincing; the word *forced* does not fit meaningfully into the sentence.
    B.   *Scholarly* research fits the meaning, but *prevented* does not fit grammatically nor meaningfully.
    C.   *Extensive* research fits the meaning, and *enabled* indicates success.
    D.   *Elementary* research would not be convincing, and *fostered* does not fit grammatically nor meaningfully.

Choice C is the correct response.

TESTING TIP:

In a question of this type, it is necessary that both words fit into the sentence in terms of meaning and grammatical form. It is possible that one word in the pair may fit while the other does not. A choice of this type would be incorrect.

2-10A. DETERMINING VOCABULARY IN CONTEXT

Activity: Use the testing tip in order to find the best word pair for each sentence.

1. The homeowner had always _____ his beautiful view of the lake until the highrise building was put up and _____ his view.
   A. despised – limited
   B. valued – enhanced
   C. cherished – embellished
   D. appreciated – obstructed

2. As the European sports car rounded the turn and headed toward the finish line, it _____ as the competition _____, resulting in Joe's first win.
   A. slowed – fell
   B. sped – slowed
   C. sputtered – raced
   D. accelerated – lagged

3. Because of the child's _____ behavior, she was _____ to the backyard for the rest of the afternoon.
   A. inappropriate – confined
   B. complaining – continued
   C. gracious – limited
   D. model – assigned

4. The receptionist called to _____ my appointment, and I _____ the time and date before hanging up the phone.
   A. conform – recorded
   B. establish – embellished
   C. cancel – recorded
   D. confirm – verified

5. As the attorney proceeded to _____ the witness, the jury _____ on the defendant's innocence.
   A. question – voted
   B. interrogate – speculated
   C. judge – commented
   D. confuse – despaired

6. Given the two superior choices, the student found himself in a pleasant _____ knowing that he would _____ from either outcome.
   A. dilemma – benefit
   B. disaster – fail
   C. place – despair
   D. quagmire – gain

2-10A. *Continued*

7. The decision to irrigate the fields was _____ and _____ increased profits from the sale of the crops.
   A. desirable – limited
   B. facetious – caused
   C. unreasonable – allowed
   D. beneficial – yielded

8. New photographic processes _____ the quality of reproducing _____ photographs and have won rave reviews with the consumers.
   A. distorted – old
   B. enhanced – antique
   C. limited – new
   D. detracted – classic

9. The security system was installed to _____ the intrusion of _____ into the vacant house.
   A. warn – robbers
   B. announce – insects
   C. promote – thieves
   D. monitor – burglars

10. As the flight was nearing its _____, the plane began to _____ in preparation for landing.
    A. takeoff – ascend
    B. crest – accelerate
    C. end – lift
    D. destination – descend

Extension: Create five original sentences like those above and provide four possible word pair answers. Indicate your correct choice and explain why it is correct.

Name_____ Date_____

2-11. A STRATEGY FOR TAKING IN-CLASS TESTS

When taking a test in the classroom on a unit of study, you may be called upon to define a content-related term. Below is a strategy for defining the meaning of such words.

Example: Define the term *triangle.*

Possible Response: A *triangle* is a geometric shape. It is a closed figure and has three sides. In some cases the three sides may be equal, and in others the sides can be of differing lengths. The triangular shape can be seen in the pyramids of Egypt, in the shape of yield signs on our roadways, and within many architectual designs.

Explanation: In this definition, the term is included *(triangle);* the category to which it belongs *(geometric shape);* the characteristics that make it distinctive *(closed figure with three sides);* and where you may find examples of it in the world *(pyramids, yield signs,* and *architecture).*

TESTING TIP:

When asked to define a term, provide information that fully explains the term. Your definition may include the following: term, category to which it belongs, its distinctive characteristics, and where one might find it.

Sample Term: Unicycle

Category: Bicycle

Distinctive Characteristics: One Wheel

Where Found: Circus Acts, Bike Stores

Sample Definition:

A unicycle is a special kind of bicycle. Unlike others in the category, it has only one wheel. It is often seen in circus acts and can be purchased in many bicycle shops.

Name_____ Date_____

2-11A. TAKING IN-CLASS TESTS

Activity: For each term presented, complete the information requested. Then use this information to write a well-developed definition for the term.

1. Term: *square*

   Category: _____

   Distinctive Characteristics: _____

   _____

   Where Seen or Found: _____

   _____

   Definition: _____

   _____

   _____

   _____

   _____

2. Term: *biography*

   Category: _____

   Distinctive Characteristics: _____

   _____

   Where Seen or Found: _____

   _____

   Definition: _____

   _____

   _____

   _____

   _____

3. Term: *apple*

   Category: _____

   Distinctive Characteristics: _____

   _____

   Where Seen or Found: _____

   _____

   Definition: _____

   _____

   _____

   _____

   _____

2-11A. Continued

4. Term: *isthmus*

   Category: _____

   Distinctive Characteristics: _____

   _____

   Where Seen or Found: _____

   _____

   Definition: _____

   _____

   _____

   _____

   _____

   _____

5. Term: *mammal*

   Category: _____

   Distinctive Characteristics: _____

   _____

   Where Seen or Found: _____

   _____

   Definition: _____

   _____

   _____

   _____

   _____

   _____

6. Term: *sandal*

   Category: _____

   Distinctive Characteristics: _____

   _____

   Where Seen or Found: _____

   _____

   Definition: _____

   _____

   _____

   _____

   _____

2-11B. TAKING IN-CLASS TESTS

Activity: For each term presented, complete the information requested. Then use this information to write a well-developed definition for the term.

1. Term: *tree*

   Category: _____

   Distinctive Characteristics: _____

   _____

   Where Seen or Found: _____

   _____

   Definition: _____

   _____

   _____

   _____

   _____

   _____

2. Term: *computer*

   Category: _____

   Distinctive Characteristics: _____

   _____

   Where Seen or Found: _____

   _____

   Definition: _____

   _____

   _____

   _____

   _____

3. Term: *elephant*

   Category: _____

   Distinctive Characteristics: _____

   _____

   Where Seen or Found: _____

   _____

   Definition: _____

   _____

   _____

   _____

   _____

4. Term: *canyon*

   Category: _____

   Distinctive Characteristics: _____

   _____

   Where Seen or Found: _____

   _____

   Definition: _____

   _____

   _____

   _____

   _____

5. Term: *hero*

   Category: _____

   Distinctive Characteristics: _____

   _____

   Where Seen or Found: _____

   _____

   Definition: _____

   _____

   _____

   _____

   _____

6. Term: *snow*

   Category: _____

   Distinctive Characteristics: _____

   _____

   Where Seen or Found: _____

   _____

   Definition: _____

   _____

   _____

   _____

   _____

2-12. A STRATEGY FOR WRITING SENTENCES THAT SHOW UNDERSTANDING

When taking a test in the classroom on a unit of study, you may be called upon to use a content-related term in a sentence. Below is a strategy for writing a sentence that shows you understand the term and how it is used.

Example: Define the term *revolt*.

Sentence: The colonists chose to revolt and stand up for their rights and protest when the King of England decided to tax the colonists on their tea.

Explanation: In this sentence there are some clues as to the meaning of *revolt*. The words *stand up for their rights and protest* tell us that *revolt* means to show strong opposition toward some position.

TESTING TIP:

When asked to use a term in a sentence that shows your understanding of that term, provide clues within the sentence to help the reader make sense of the word.

2-12A. WRITING SENTENCES THAT SHOW UNDERSTANDING

Activity: For each term presented, write a sentence that uses the term correctly and provides clues as to the term's meaning.

1. Term: *pollute*

    Sentence:_____

    _____

    _____

    _____

    _____

2. Term: *initiate*

    Sentence:_____

    _____

    _____

    _____

    _____

3. Term: *fluctuate*

    Sentence:_____

    _____

    _____

    _____

    _____

4. Term: *resolve*

    Sentence:_____

    _____

    _____

    _____

    _____

5. Term: *witness*

    Sentence:_____

    _____

    _____

    _____

    _____

Name_____ Date_____

2-12B. WRITING SENTENCES THAT SHOW UNDERSTANDING

Activity: For each term presented, write a sentence that uses the term correctly and provides clues as to the term's meaning.

1. Term: *recycle*

   Sentence:_____

   _____

   _____

   _____

   _____

2. Term: *exaggeration*

   Sentence:_____

   _____

   _____

   _____

   _____

3. Term: *niche*

   Sentence:_____

   _____

   _____

   _____

   _____

4. Term: *symbolize*

   Sentence:_____

   _____

   _____

   _____

   _____

5. Term: *espionage*

   Sentence:_____

   _____

   _____

   _____

2-13. A STRATEGY FOR TAKING MULTIPLE-CHOICE TESTS

Tests in the subject areas, especially science and social studies, often focus on vocabulary. A full understanding of the vocabulary is often necessary to develop concepts in these areas. Many teacher-made tests present vocabulary in multiple-choice format. In this type of test, vocabulary terms and definitions may be presented for you to match the term with its correct definition.

Example: The study of living things is called

    A. geology.
    B. psychology.
    C. zoology.
    D. biology.

Explanation: The word part *ology* means *the study of,* so each of these terms fits the first part of the definition given. *Geo* refers to *the earth,* as in geography, geophysics, and geometry. *Psych* refers to *the mind,* as in psychosomatic, psychoanalysis, and psychotherapy. *Zoo* refers to *animals,* as in a zoo, zooplankton, and zoography. *Bio* refers to *life,* as in biography (the story of a person's life) and biome (a community of living things in one ecological region). In this case, choice D is the best answer. Psychology might be a choice because psychology is the study of the mind, and humans are living things, but reading further will show you that choice D is a better answer. Zoology might also be a first choice because animals are living things, but again, choice D is a better answer.

Name_____ Date_____

2-13A. TAKING MULTIPLE-CHOICE TESTS

Activity: Read the passage below. Then select the best choice for each vocabulary term presented in multiple-choice form.

Cells

The cell is the basic unit that makes up all living things. The nucleus is the structure within the cell that controls the cell's activities. Cytoplasm is the jellylike material enclosed within the cell by the cell membrane. The cell membrane controls the passage of materials, such as food, gases, and wastes in and out of the cell. Mitochondria produce energy for the cell to perform its activities. Mitochondria are most common in cells such as those that make up heart muscle, since these cells must work constantly. The endoplasmic reticulum is a system of membranes through the cytoplasm that provide passageways for the movement of materials throughout the cell. Ribosomes are structures on which proteins are made. The Golgi apparatus prepares materials for secretion from the cell. Storage areas within the cell are called vacuoles. Vacuoles may hold food, water, or waste materials. Lysosomes are digestive enzymes that help break down starches, lipids, and proteins. Lysosomes also digest disease-causing bacteria and destroy worn-out parts of the cell. Even though cells are tiny, their structure and functions are complex.

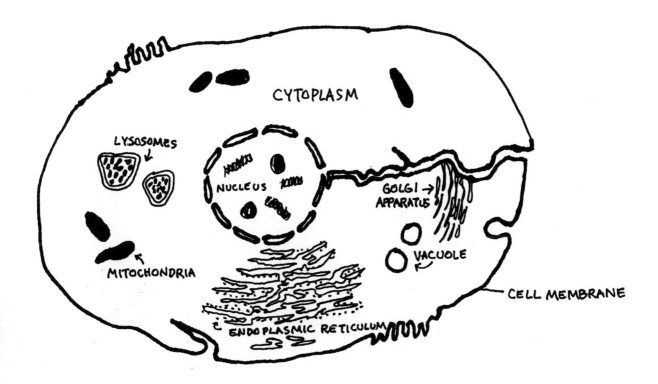

2-13A. Continued

1. All living things are made up of
   A. cytoplasm.
   B. vacuoles.
   C. cells.
   D. mitochondria.

2. Within a cell, proteins are made on
   A. lysosomes.
   B. vacuoles.
   C. Golgi apparatus.
   D. ribosomes.

3. Mitochondria would be found in greater numbers in
   A. cells in the lungs.
   B. cells in the fingernail.
   C. muscle cells in the arm.
   D. cells in the eye.

4. The passage of materials into the cell is controlled by the
   A. nucleus.
   B. cell membrane.
   C. endoplasmic reticulum.
   D. vacuoles.

5. The jellylike material within the cell is called the
   A. endoplasmic reticulum.
   B. cyctoplasm.
   C. lysosomes.
   D. cell membrane.

2-14. A STRATEGY FOR TAKING MATCHING TESTS

Tests in the subject areas, especially science and social studies, often focus on vocabulary. A full understanding of the vocabulary is often necessary to develop concepts in these areas. Many teacher-made tests present vocabulary in multiple-choice format. Matching tests are a variation of a multiple-choice test. In this type of test, vocabulary terms and definitions may be presented for you to match the term with its correct definition.

TESTING TIP:

Use notecards to help you study for a matching test. Write the vocabulary term on one side and its definition on the other. When you study, have someone else ask you the words while you give the definitions. Then, have someone read you the definitions while you supply the vocabulary term.

2-14A. TAKING MATCHING TESTS

Activity: Read the passage. Then write the letter of the correct definition in front of each Greek god's name.

The Gods of Olympus

On Mount Olympus, the gods ruled over heaven and earth. Zeus was the god of thunder, the mightiest of all the gods. As Zeus sat on his throne, he kept a bucket of thunderbolts beside him. Hera was Zeus's queen and the goddess of marriage. Aphrodite, the goddess of love, had a playful son named Eros. Eros flew about with a bow and arrows of love which he happily shot into the hearts of mortals causing them to immediately fall helplessly in love. Ares was the god of war, tall and handsome, but cruel and vain. Ares loved a battle, but he did not care who won as long as it was a bloody battle. Poseidon was the god of the sea, ruling over all the oceans. Athena was the goddess of wisdom and was Zeus's favorite child. Athena led armies, but only for just causes. During peace, Athena taught mortals many wonderful things. Apollo was the god of light and music; Dionysus was the god of wine. Artemis was the goddess of the hunt and brought good hunting to those she favored. Hestia was the goddess of the hearth who took care of the sacred fire on Mount Olympus and was honored by every hearth on earth. Hades was the god of the underworld who ruled over the dead. Hephaestus was the god of fire; Hermes was the herald, and Demeter was the goddess of the harvest. The gods could not die and enjoyed interfering in the lives of humans. They often appeared on earth, both solving and causing problems for mortals.

1. Apollo		A.	god of harvest
2. Athena		B.	Aphrodite's son
3. Zeus		C.	god of the sea
4. Ares		D.	fought for just causes
5. Dionysus		E.	god of music
6. Poseidon		F.	mightiest god
7. Demeter		G.	god of war
8. Eros		H.	god of wine

2-15. A STRATEGY FOR TAKING FILL-IN-THE-BLANK TESTS

Tests in the subject areas, especially science and social studies, often focus on vocabulary. A full understanding of the vocabulary is often necessary to develop concepts in these areas. Sentence completion or fill-in-the-blank tests rely on your knowledge of the vocabulary. Use context clues where possible to help you determine the terms being asked.

TESTING TIP:

Use notecards to help you study for a vocabulary test. Write the vocabulary term on one side and its definition on the other. When you study, have someone else ask you the words while you give the definitions. Then, have someone read you the definitions while you supply the vocabulary term.

2-15A. TAKING FILL-IN-THE-BLANK TESTS

Activity: Read the test items below. Then fill in the correct responses on the lines provided. These items are based on general knowledge of the United States. You may use an atlas as needed.

1. The capital of the United States is _____.

2. The Great Lakes are _____,

   _____, _____,

   _____, _____.

3. The smallest state is _____.

4. Florida is bordered by the states of _____ and

   _____.

5. The states that border the Pacific Ocean are _____,

   _____, and _____.

6. The capital of Montana is _____.

7. The Grand Canyon is located in which state? _____

8. Yellowstone National Park is located in which state? _____

9. The Great Salt Lake is located in which state? _____

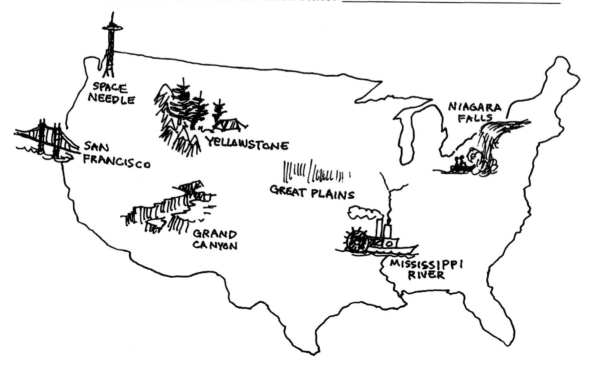

2-16. A STRATEGY FOR DECODING DINOSAURS

Prefixes and suffixes have meanings that can be used to decode unfamiliar words. Knowing the meanings of common prefixes and suffixes will enable you to determine the meaning or partial meaning of unknown words.

Example: In the quiet concert hall, the *vociferous* child was a disturbing distraction.

Explanation: The suffix *ous* means full of. The root *voc* means voice. Therefore, you may be able to deduce that vociferous means full of voice or noisy.

TESTING TIP:

Knowing some common word parts may help you to know the partial meaning of an unfamiliar word. Use this information as a clue to help you make your best guess about the meaning of the whole word.

Name_____ Date_____

2-16A. DECODING DINOSAURS

Activity: Below is a chart of prefixes and suffixes used to name dinosaurs. Use this chart to help you decode the meaning of the dinosaur names listed.

PREFIXES

brachio – arm
bronte – thunder
cory – helmet
dino – terrible
diplo – double
mono – one
orni – bird
ova – egg
pachy – thick
proto – first

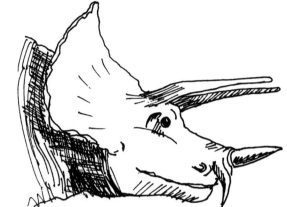

TRI = THREE   CERATOPS = HORNED FACE

SUFFIXES

cephalic – head
ceratops – horned face
derma – skin
gnathus – jaw
mimus – imitator
raptor – thief
saurus – lizard

1. Brachiosaurus

_____

2. Brontesaurus

_____

3. Corythosaurus

_____

4. Dinosaur

_____

5. Ornithomimus

_____

6. Pachycephalosaurus

_____

7. Protoceratops

_____

8. Ovaraptor

_____

Extension: Using the chart above, list at least five words you know that contain at least one of the word parts. Then give the meaning for each word.

2-17. A STRATEGY FOR DECODING UNFAMILIAR WORDS

Prefixes, suffixes, and roots have meanings that can be used to decode unfamiliar words. Knowing the meanings of common word parts will enable you to determine the meaning or partial meaning of unknown words. Prefixes appear at the beginning of a word. They are usually a syllable that adds to or changes the meaning of the root word. Suffixes appear at the end of a word. They are usually an ending that may change the form of the word, such as from a verb to a noun, or may change the inflection of the word.

Example: The word *linguist* means *a person skilled in a language.*
        The word *bilinguist* means *a person skilled in two languages.*
        The word *multilinguist* means *a person skilled in many languages.*

Explanation: The prefix *bi* means *two* and the prefix *multi* means *many.* The use of these prefixes changes the meaning of the word by indicating the number of languages known.

TESTING TIP:

If you encounter an unfamiliar word, check to see if it contains a prefix, suffix, or root that you recognize as part of a known word. Try to think of other words containing that word part to see if you can determine the meaning of the word part. Then use this meaning to help you figure out the meaning or partial meaning of the unfamiliar word.

Example: Imagine that the word *subaqueous* is an unfamiliar word.

        You may recognize the prefix *sub* from *submarine, subordinate, subscript.* A submarine goes under the ocean, a subordinate is a person under the authority of another, and a subscript is written under the line. The common meaning among these three words is *under.*

        You may recognize the suffix *ous* from *jealous, dangerous, hilarious.* These three words are all adjectives ending in *ous.*

        You may recognize the root *aqua* from *aquatic, aquarium, aquaplane.* These three words all have to do with *water.*

        Putting together the meanings of the word parts will help you conclude that *subaqueous* describes something as *being under water.*

2-17A. DECODING UNFAMILIAR WORDS

Activity: Write the meaning for each word. Then use the meanings to determine the meaning of the word part common to each group.

1. antiabortion _____
   antibacterial _____
   antifreeze _____
   anti means _____

2. co-driver _____
   co-owner _____
   co-worker _____
   co means _____

3. autobiography _____
   autograph _____
   autofocus _____
   auto means _____

4. ex-convict _____
   ex-president _____
   ex-husband _____
   ex means _____

5. geography _____
   geology _____
   geophysics _____
   geo means _____

6. inaction _____
   incapable _____
   invisible _____
   in means _____

Name_____ Date_____

2-17A. Continued

7. misconduct _____

    misinterpret _____

    mistrust _____

      mis means _____

8. redefine _____

    reboot _____

    retrial _____

      re means _____

9. transport _____

    transcontinental _____

    transfer _____

      trans means _____

10. interstate _____

    interim _____

    interact _____

      inter means _____

Name_____ Date_____

2-17B. DECODING UNFAMILIAR WORDS

Activity: Write the meaning for each word. Then use the meanings to determine the meaning of the word part common to each group.

1. orthodontics _____

   orthodox _____

   orthology _____

   ortho means _____

2. semicircle _____

   semifinal _____

   semi-yearly _____

   semi means _____

3. theology _____

   theocracy _____

   theosophy _____

   theo means _____

4. pseudonym _____

   pseudo-science _____

   pseudograph _____

   pseudo means _____

5. premature _____

   predetermine _____

   precede _____

   pre means _____

6. quadruple _____

   quadrant _____

   quadrangle _____

   quad means _____

2-17B. Continued

7. return   _____

    redefine   _____

    reinstate   _____

      re means   _____

8. triangle   _____

    tricycle   _____

    triceratops   _____

      tri means   _____

9. anthropoid   _____

    anthropologist   _____

    anthromorphic   _____

      anthro means   _____

10. disagree   _____

    disbelief   _____

    discomfort   _____

      dis means   _____

2-18. ANOTHER STRATEGY FOR DECODING UNFAMILIAR WORDS

Prefixes, suffixes, and roots have meanings that can be used to decode unfamiliar words. Knowing the meanings of common word parts will enable you to determine the meaning or partial meaning of unknown words. Prefixes appear at the beginning of a word. They are usually a syllable that adds to or changes the meaning of the root word. Suffixes appear at the end of a word. They are usually an ending that may change the form of the word, such as from a verb to a noun, or may change the inflection of the word.

Example: The word *linguist* means *a person who studies languages.*
The word *biologist* means *a person who studies living things.*
The word *geologist* means *a person who studies the earth.*

Explanation: The suffix *ist* means *person.*

DIA DUIT

ITALIAN
SPANISH
FRENCH
IRISH

LINGUIST

BIOLOGIST

GEOLOGIST

TESTING TIP:

If you encounter an unfamiliar word, check to see if it contains a prefix, suffix, or root that you recognize as part of a known word. Try to think of other words containing that word part to see if you can determine the meaning of the word part. Then use this meaning to help you figure out the meaning or partial meaning of the unfamiliar word.

Example: Imagine that the word *subaqueous* is an unfamiliar word.

You may recognize the prefix *sub* from *submarine, subordinate, subscript.* A submarine goes under the ocean, a subordinate is a person under the authority of another, and a subscript is written under the line. The common meaning among these three words is *under.*

You may recognize the suffix *ous* from *jealous, dangerous, hilarious.* These three words are all adjectives ending in *ous.*

You may recognize the root *aqua* from *aquatic, aquarium, aquaplane.* These three words all have to do with *water.*

Putting together the meanings of the word parts will help you conclude that *subaqueous* describes something as *being under water.*

Name_____ Date_____

2-18A. DECODING UNFAMILIAR WORDS

Activity: Write the meaning for each word. Then use the meanings to determine the meaning of the word part common to each group.

1. capable

_____

believable

_____

changeable

_____

   able means _____

2. beautiful

_____

sorrowful

_____

pitiful

_____

   ful means _____

3. prosperous

_____

melodious

_____

industrious

_____

   ous means_____

4. fearless

_____

hopeless

_____

penniless

_____

   less means _____

5. heroism

_____

patriotism

_____

alcoholism

_____

   ism means _____

2-18A. Continued

6. kindness

_____

bitterness

_____

darkness

_____

ness means _____

7. geology

_____

biology

_____

archaeology

_____

logy means _____

8. foolish

_____

impish

_____

sluggish

_____

ish means _____

9. excitement

_____

accomplishment

_____

ornament

_____

ment means _____

10. arrogance

_____

appearance

_____

riddance

_____

ance means _____

© 1997 by John Wiley & Sons, Inc.

COMPREHENSION

Standardized and classroom tests often use similar vocabulary when presenting test questions and directions. Familiarity with these words and phrasings can be helpful when taking such tests. Increased understanding of these words and phrases will help you in responding to such test questions.

Here are some of the common directions used on tests for testing reading comprehension:

- Read each question and decide which one of the choices best answers the question.
- What is the main idea of the passage?
- Which of the following is the best summary?
- Which of the following happened first?
- The author of the passage wants you to:
- Which of the following sentences is an opinion?
- The main purpose of the passage is:
- Which of the following is not mentioned in the passage?
- Which of the following would be the most accurate title of the passage?
- The author's attitude can best be described as:
- The author is primarily concerned with discussing:
- Which of the following reflects fact rather than opinion?
- Which of the following best states the theme of the passage?
- The tone of the last sentence in the passage can best be described as:
- The primary purpose of the passage is to:
- The author implies _____ by:
- The author uses the example of _____ in order to:
- What does the word _____ mean in the passage?
- The statement _____ is best interpreted as conveying:
- The author uses the words _____ to express:
- The author includes _____ to emphasize:
- The last sentence means that _____.
- Which words tell that . . .?
- The first paragraph tells the reader . . .
- The author probably included the last sentence of the second paragraph to show that . . .
- The last sentence means that . . .
- In this passage what tone does the writer use?
- This passage is an example of which type of writing?
- This passage mainly describes . . .
- There is enough information in this passage to show that . . .
- Which words tell that _____ was _____?

2-19. A STRATEGY FOR IDENTIFYING THE MAIN IDEA

The main idea in a passage is often stated in a topic sentence that most often appears at the beginning or end of the passage. To help identify the main idea, try to answer the following questions after reading the passage:

Who or what is the passage about?
What happened?
When?
Where?
How?
Why?

Sometimes not enough information is given to answer all the questions, but they generally will help you summarize the main idea.

Example: Emperor penguin chicks hatch into extreme conditions as they begin their lives. On an ice shelf in the Antarctic, a penguin chick faces an average temperature of –4° F with winds of 50 miles per hour. There is hardly any light during the Antarctic winter. Emperor penguins breed in this inhospitable environment because there are no predators to eat the babies. For the penguin, the advantages of safety and a plentiful food supply in the surrounding ocean waters outweigh the disadvantages of the weather conditions.

Explanation: Who or what is the passage about? *Emperor penguins*
What happened? *Hatch chicks in extreme weather conditions*
When? *Winter*
Where? *Antarctic*
How?
Why? *No predators, but plentiful food*

Main idea choices:
A. Winter in the Antarctic is extreme with temperatures of –4° F and winds of 50 miles per hour.
B. There are no predators of Emperor penguin chicks in the Antarctic.
C. Emperor penguin chicks are hatched into severe conditions that afford them safety from predators and plentiful food.
D. Penguin chicks cannot see at birth because it is dark in the Antarctic winter.

Choice C is correct because it includes the main ideas presented in the passage. It also includes most of the information contained in the answers to the questions listed above.

TESTING TIP:

Learn the questions and then use their answers to check against the main idea choices.

2-19A. IDENTIFYING THE MAIN IDEA

Activity: Read each passage. Answer the questions and then choose the main idea from the choices listed.

1. A kangaroo is a marsupial, a pouched mammal that has its babies develop for only a short time inside the mother's womb and for a more extended time in the mother's pouch. A newborn kangaroo is smaller than your thumb with no fur and closed eyes. The newborn must make its way through its mother's fur to the pouch where it can begin to nurse on milk. During the next few months inside the pouch, the baby will grow fur and its eyes will open. Its limbs develop and it grows larger. After about six months in the pouch, the baby looks like its parents, only smaller. It begins to leave the pouch for short periods to graze on plants. By ten months, the young kangaroo is too large to fit inside the pouch, but it still puts its head inside to drink milk. Finally, at about fourteen months, the young kangaroo is independent and leaves its mother to join the other kangaroos in the mob. By the age of two or three, the young kangaroo will start its own family.

Who or what is the passage about?

_____

What happened?

_____

When?

_____

Where?

_____

How?

_____

Why?

_____

- A.   Kangaroos are marsupials.
- B.   Baby kangaroos stay in the pouch for six months and stay with their mothers for another eight months.
- C.   A newborn kangaroo is tiny and helpless at birth and then develops inside its mother's pouch until it is too large to fit.
- D.   A marsupial is a pouched mammal that reaches adulthood in two to three years.

2-19A. Continued

2. The cheetah uses its incredible speed to chase down its prey. First, the cheetah slowly and quietly stalks a gazelle, impala, or wildebeest. Then, reaching speeds of about 65 miles per hour, the cheetah sprints after its victim. As it overtakes its prey, the cheetah bites the underside of the animal's throat, shutting the windpipe to kill it. Unlike other cats, the cheetah does not have retractable claws which can be withdrawn to keep them sharp and protected. Therefore, the cheetah has short, blunt claws that are not useful for killing or scratching. Speed is the cheetah's great advantage as a hunter. Open areas allow the cheetah to use its speed to its fullest. If the cheetah does not overtake its prey during a quick sprint, it quickly gives up. Lacking stamina, the cheetah cannot run long distances. At great speeds, the cheetah cannot change direction easily so if the prey swerves, it may escape. Even with its tremendous speed, the cheetah is successful in catching its prey only about half the time.

Who or what is the passage about?

_____

What happened?

_____

When?

_____

Where?

_____

How?

_____

Why?

_____

A. Cheetahs kill gazelles, impalas, and wildebeests as their prey.
B. Speed is the cheetah's greatest advantage as a predator.
C. The cheetah bites to kill its prey because its claws are not sharp.
D. The cheetah will chase its prey for long distances, rarely giving up.

2-20. ANOTHER STRATEGY FOR IDENTIFYING THE MAIN IDEA

The main idea in a passage is often stated in a topic sentence that most often appears at the beginning or end of the passage. To help identify the main idea, try to answer the following questions after reading the passage:

Who or what is the passage about?
What happened?
When?
Where?
How?
Why?

Sometimes not enough information is given to answer all the questions, but they generally will help you summarize the main idea.

Example: In 1973, NASA launched Mariner 10 which traveled to Mercury and, in 1974, gave us new information about the closest planet to the sun. The surface of this small planet is barren and cratered. There is evidence of former volcanic activity, and huge craters formed by tremendous impact. The thin rocky surface was wrinkled into tremendous ridges as the planet beneath cooled and shrank. The surface can be compared to the skin of a shrunken old apple. Mercury has less rock on its surface than the other rocky planets. Many astronomers believe much of Mercury's rock was blasted into space by the impact of giant asteroids. Mariner 10 is the only spacecraft to have visited Mercury, giving us a better view of this battered planet, but leaving many questions unanswered.

Explanation: After reading the passage, answer these questions to help you identify the main idea. Then, use the information in your answers to write a one-sentence statement summarizing the main idea.

Who or what is the passage about? *Mercury*
What happened? *Mariner 10 visited Mercury and found craters, ridges, and barren rocky landscape*
When? *1974*
Where? *Space*
How?
Why? *To learn more about the surface of the planet*

In 1974, Mariner 10 visited Mercury, finding craters, ridges, and a barren rocky landscape, and adding to our knowledge about the planet.

TESTING TIP:

Learn the questions and then use their answers to form your own main idea statement before checking it against the main idea choices given on the test.

2-20A. IDENTIFYING THE MAIN IDEA

Activity: Read each passage. Answer the questions and then write a one-sentence statement summarizing the main idea.

1. In Greek mythology, Hercules is known for his strength and courage. When still a baby, he strangled two great serpents sent to kill him. In his youth, he killed a lion with his bare hands. He then wore its skin as a cloak and its head as a helmet. He faced Hydra, a monster with nine heads. When one was cut off, two others grew in its place, but Hercules sealed each neck with a burning torch to prevent more heads from appearing. When challenged to clean the Augean stables, which had not been cleaned in 30 years, he changed the course of two rivers to flow through the stables and carry away the filth. Through his adventures, Hercules always demonstrated intelligence, strength, and courage. He was a hero greatly admired by the Greeks and by readers today.

Who or what is the passage about?

_____

What happened?

_____

When?

_____

Where?

_____

How?

_____

Why?

_____

Main Idea Sentence:

_____

_____

2-20A. IDENTIFYING THE MAIN IDEA, CONTINUED

2. In 1780, Benedict Arnold asked General George Washington to give him command of West Point. As a soldier, Arnold realized the strategic importance of West Point. At this time, General Arnold was a respected soldier in the patriot army. No one knew that his bride, Peggy Shippen, had been successful in convincing Arnold that the British cause was right and just. In September, 1780, Arnold was discovered as a traitor who had given a British spy plans on how to attack West Point and how Arnold would surrender it. Although the spy, Major John Andre, was hanged, Benedict Arnold escaped to Britain. His treason made him lose the respect of both Americans and British. He died in Britain a sad and lonely man 20 years later.

Who or what is the passage about?

_____

What happened?

_____

When?

_____

Where?

_____

How?

_____

Why?

_____

Main Idea Sentence:

_____

_____

Extension: Choose several passages from a textbook to read. Then answer the questions above and write a main idea sentence for each passage.

Name_____ Date_____

2-21. A STRATEGY FOR ORGANIZING INFORMATION

The main idea in a passage is often stated in a topic sentence that most often appears at the beginning or end of the passage. Supporting details are also contained in the passage that explain and give additional information. To help you deal with information in a passage, draw a semantic map to organize the main ideas, subtopics, and details. A semantic map will help you learn to organize information and remember details.

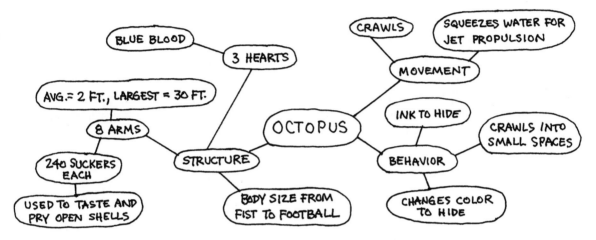

Explanation: Above is a semantic map about the octopus. *Octopus* is the subject so it appears in the center of the map. Branching out from it are the subtopics (*structure, movement,* and *behavior*). Branching out from these are the supporting details. Organizing information into this type of format will help you see which things are more important and how the information is related.

TESTING TIP:

Practicing with semantic maps helps you to organize information and see relationships. This process will help you recognize and remember details as you read.

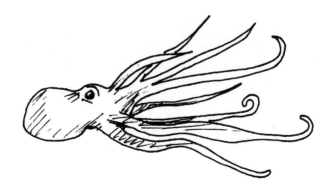

2-21A. ORGANIZING INFORMATION

Activity: Read the following passage. Then construct a semantic map to organize the information.

Spiders belong to the class Arachnids. There are about 30,000 different kinds of spiders. They all have eight legs, no antennae, eight eyes, and two body parts. Spiders are carnivores and feed mainly on insects that they catch by hunting or trapping. Poison is injected into the prey through fangs. The poison causes the prey to be paralyzed and also begins its digestion, turning it into a liquid which the spider can later suck out.

Some spiders use webs to help them catch their prey. The garden spider weaves a beautiful sticky web and then waits for insects to get caught in it. The web-casting spider spins a small, sticky web which it opens and drops on insects walking below. The hammock spider covers plants with tangled mats of web. When insects walk on the mats, they trip over the loose threads and are then attacked by the waiting spider. Other spiders just attack without using webs. The jumping spider can jump 40 times its length and land right on its prey. The wolf spider slowly stalks and then pounces on its prey. Spiders are actually very helpful in controlling insect populations.

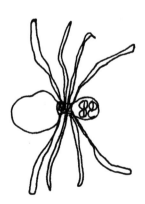

Extension: Read a passage from a textbook and then construct a semantic map to organize the information. This strategy is also useful to help you study for a test.

2-22. ANOTHER STRATEGY FOR ORGANIZING INFORMATION

The main idea in a passage is often stated in a topic sentence that most often appears at the beginning or end of the passage. Supporting details are also contained in the passage that explain and give additional information. To help you deal with information in a passage, construct a graphic organizer to show the relationship among the main ideas, subtopics, and details. A graphic organizer will help you learn to organize information and remember details.

Example of a Graphic Organizer:

VERTEBRATES					
CLASSES	AMPHIBIANS	BIRDS	FISH	MAMMALS	REPTILES
BODY COVERINGS	skin	feathers	scales	hair or fur	scales
REPRODUCTION	jelly eggs	hard-shelled eggs	eggs or live birth	live birth	leathery eggs
RESPIRATION	gills/lungs	lungs	gills	lungs	lungs

Explanation: Above is a graphic organizer about vertebrates. *Vertebrates* is the subject so it appears in the center of the organizer. Listed below it are the subtopics (*body covering, reproduction,* and *respiration*). Under each class of vertebrates is the appropriate information. Organizing information into this type of format will help you see which things are more important and how the information is related.

TESTING TIP:

Practicing with graphic organizers helps you to organize information and see relationships. This process will help you recognize and remember details as you read.

2-22A. ORGANIZING INFORMATION

Activity: Read the following passage. Then construct a graphic organizer to organize the information.

Searching the sky reveals a variety of celestial objects. The most prominent of these is the sun which happens to be a star, a ball of burning gases that gives off its own light. The night sky reveals millions of stars just like our sun. Orbiting our sun are nine planets, large bodies that revolve around a star. Many planets have smaller orbiting bodies called moons. Earth has only one moon, but Saturn may have more than twenty-six.

Our solar system includes all the bodies that orbit around our sun. There is only one star in our solar system, even though there are billions in the universe. Nine planets make up our solar system with over sixty moons orbiting those planets.

Conditions on the planets vary greatly in temperature, amount of light, composition of planet, and atmosphere. Earth is the only planet in our solar system that supports life as we know it.

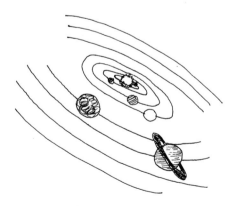

Extension: Read a passage from a textbook and then construct a semantic map to organize the information. This strategy is also useful to help you study for a test.

2-23. A THIRD STRATEGY FOR ORGANIZING INFORMATION

Sometimes information in a passage is a series of events. Organizing this kind of information into a story map can help you see exactly what happened, when it happened, and how the events are related. Cause-and-effect relationships are easily distinguished in a story map.

Example:

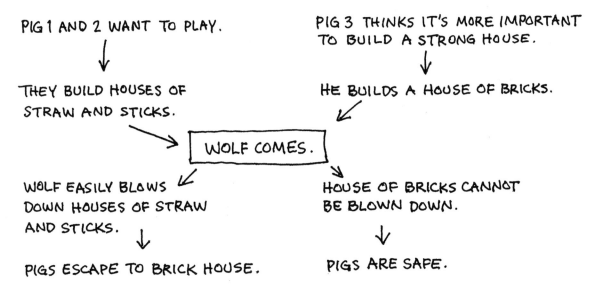

PIG 1 AND 2 WANT TO PLAY.

↓

THEY BUILD HOUSES OF STRAW AND STICKS.

PIG 3 THINKS IT'S MORE IMPORTANT TO BUILD A STRONG HOUSE.

↓

HE BUILDS A HOUSE OF BRICKS.

WOLF COMES.

WOLF EASILY BLOWS DOWN HOUSES OF STRAW AND STICKS.

↓

PIGS ESCAPE TO BRICK HOUSE.

HOUSE OF BRICKS CANNOT BE BLOWN DOWN.

↓

PIGS ARE SAFE.

Explanation: Above is a story map about the story of the Three Little Pigs. The major actions of the story are listed to show the order and to show cause and effect. This organization will help you simplify and see relationships.

TESTING TIP:

Practicing with story maps helps you to organize information and see relationships. This process will help you see the cause-and-effect relationships in the material you read.

97

2-23A. ORGANIZING INFORMATION

Activity: Read the following passage. Then construct a story map to organize the information.

On March 20, 1980, Mount St. Helens had an earthquake after no geologic activity for a period of 123 years. Following this initial earthquake was a series of smaller, frequent earthquakes and small explosions. These explosions resulted in new craters forming on the mountain. The north side of the mountaintop began to bulge, growing in size at a rate of five to six feet a day. By mid-May, the bulge was a half mile wide, more than a mile long, and had swelled out 300 feet. On May 18, Mount St. Helens erupted. The eruption began with an earthquake that caused an avalanche. The earthquake shook the bulge which broke loose as an avalanche of rock. The avalanche tore into the mountain releasing a blast of steam carrying shattered rocks at a speed of 200 miles per hour. The force of this blast leveled 150 square miles. Then Mount St. Helens began to erupt with a dark column of ash and rock rising miles into the sky. Hot flows of pumice and ash also began to flow down the volcano. These flows and the heat released by the eruption caused mudflows which also caused great destruction. After this eruption, Mount St. Helens erupted six more times in 1980.

Extension: Read a passage from a textbook. Then construct a story map to organize the information. This strategy is very useful for study purposes, too.

2-24. A STRATEGY FOR SEQUENCING IDEAS

As you read a story or other kinds of text, the author will present ideas in a logical order. To be an effective reader, you must be able to find clues that help you to understand the order. In standardized tests you are often presented with a written passage and asked to sequence the ideas as they were in the text.

TESTING TIP:

One strategy for handling questions having to do with the sequencing of ideas is to use signal words as clues. Often these words will alert you to the order of events or steps in a process. Become familiar with these words and use them to help you. Here are some commonly used signal words: *first, next, then, after, finally, before, now, during.*

2-24A. SEQUENCING IDEAS

Activity: Read the passage below. Then use the signal words to help you answer the questions that follow.

The fifth-rade trip to Sand Castles State Park will take place on Thursday, June 15. All student permission slips must be returned to the classroom teacher no later than June 10. Once all slips have been returned, students will then speak with Mrs. Smithson about the lunch details. This is important as the students will be having a picnic lunch, with each person contributing some part of the day's lunch.

Many activities are planned for the day at Sand Castles State Park. Upon arrival, the students will be greeted by the state park ranger who will present a short film describing the park's habitats and wildlife. Following the presentation, the group will take a short hike to the waterfall area of the park. During the visit to the waterfall area, the students will learn how the falls were formed many millions of years ago. Next it will be on to the Sand Castle Dune, a land formation for which the park was named. Before reaching this area, however, the students will pass through a small bird sanctuary in which many rare birds make their homes.

Buses for this trip will leave school promptly at 9:00 A.M. In order that we can leave on time, all students must be seated in the auditorium no later than 8:30 A.M. so that attendance can be taken and last-minute announcements made. The buses will return to school no later than 4:00 P.M.

2-24A. Continued

1. On the day of the trip, what time must students be at school?
   A. 9:00 A.M.
   B. 8:15 A.M.
   C. 8:30 A.M.
   D. 4:00 P.M.

2. What will happen between 8:30 and 9:00 A.M. the morning of the trip?
   A. A film presentation will be made.
   B. The park ranger will meet us at school.
   C. Attendance will be taken and last-minute announcements will be made.
   D. Permission slips will be collected.

3. Upon arrival at Sand Castles State Park and following the film presentation, the students will:
   A. eat lunch.
   B. visit the souvenir stand.
   C. hike to the waterfalls area.
   D. board the bus and return to school.

4. All students must have their permission slips returned to school by:
   A. 9:00 A.M.
   B. June 15.
   C. the morning of the actual trip.
   D. June 10.

5. Planning for the picnic lunch will begin:
   A. on June 15.
   B. after all signed permission slips have been returned.
   C. before permission slips go home.
   D. between 8:30 and 9:00 A.M. on June 15.

Extension: Generate an original passage like the one above. Include signal words within your passage to help emphasize the order of events. Then construct five possible test questions that focus on the sequence of happenings along with the possible answer choices.

2-25. ANOTHER STRATEGY FOR SEQUENCING IDEAS

As you read a story or other kinds of text, the author will present ideas in a logical order. To be an effective reader, you must be able to find clues that help you to understand the order. In standardized tests you are often presented with a written passage and asked to sequence the ideas as they were in the text.

TESTING TIP:

One strategy for handling questions having to do with the sequencing of ideas is to use signal words as clues. Often these words will alert you to the order of events or steps in a process. Become familiar with these words and use them to help you. Here are some commonly used signal words: *first, next, then, after, finally, before, now, during.*

Many tests require you to sequence a series of steps or statements in the correct order. Frequently, the test question will contain four or five statements each labeled with a letter or a number. Your task is to select the correct pattern of letters or numbers to match the content of the passage. It is often helpful to determine the first and/or last item and see which answer choice(s) begins and/or ends with that letter or number. You can then automatically eliminate any answer choices that begin with a different number or letter. This will help you save valuable testing time.

Name_____ Date_____

2-25A. SEQUENCING IDEAS

Activity: Read the passage below. Then use the signal words to help you answer the questions that follow. Remember to use the test-taking strategy to help save you time.

The fifth-grade trip to Sand Castles State Park will take place on Thursday, June 15. All student permission slips must be returned to the classroom teacher no later than June 10. Once all slips have been returned, students will then speak with Mrs. Smithson about the lunch details. This is important as the students will be having a picnic lunch, with each person contributing some part of the day's lunch.

Many activities are planned for the day at Sand Castles State Park. Upon arrival, the students will be greeted by the state park ranger who will present a short film describing the park's habitats and wildlife. Following the presentation, the group will take a short hike to the waterfall area of the park. During the visit to the waterfall area, the students will learn how the falls were formed many millions of years ago. Next it will be on to the Sand Castle Dune, a land formation for which the park was named. Before reaching this area, however, the students will pass through a small bird sanctuary in which many rare birds make their homes.

Buses for this trip will leave school promptly at 9:00 A.M. In order that we can leave on time, all students must be seated in the auditorium no later than 8:30 A.M. so that attendance can be taken and last-minute announcements made. The buses will return to school no later than 4:00 P.M.

2-25A. Continued

1. In what order did the answers to the following questions appear in the passage?
    1. When is the trip scheduled to take place?
    2. When will the buses return to school?
    3. When will the students meet with the ranger?
    4. When are the signed permission slips due back to school?
    5. Where will the students go following the film presentation?

    A. 1, 3, 5, 2, 4
    B. 2, 5, 3, 4, 1
    C. 1, 2, 5, 4, 3
    D. 1, 4, 3, 5, 2

2. In what order will the following events happen according to the passage?
    1. buses will return to school
    2. planning for the picnic lunch will begin
    3. attendance will be taken
    4. a visit to the Dune will take place
    5. last-minute announcements will be made

    A. 2, 3, 5, 4, 1
    B. 1, 2, 5, 4, 3
    C. 2, 5, 3, 4, 1
    D. 1, 4, 3, 5, 2

3. In what order will the following events happen according to the passage?
    1. ranger explains the wildlife habitat
    2. permission slips are due
    3. attendance will be taken
    4. a visit to the Dune will take place
    5. the date of the trip is announced

    A. 1, 2, 5, 4, 3
    B. 3, 1, 4, 5, 2
    C. 5, 2, 1, 4, 3
    D. 5, 2, 4, 1, 3

Reflection: In the space below, explain what strategy(ies) you used to choose the correct answer. Be sure to explain how the strategy(ies) helped you to choose your answer.

Extension: Using the information found in the passage, construct a schedule listing all the times and events for the day.

2-26. A STRATEGY FOR DRAWING CONCLUSIONS

As you read a story or other kinds of text, the author will present ideas. To be an effective reader, you must be able to read the information presented and piece the information together in order to draw conclusions. In standardized tests you are often presented with a written passage and asked to draw conclusions by combining pieces of information found in the passage.

TESTING TIP:

One strategy for drawing conclusions is to read the test questions first. Then read through the passage looking for specific information that can help you draw a conclusion.

2-26A. DRAWING CONCLUSIONS

Activity: Read the passage below. Then consider the questions that follow and select the best answer based upon the information found in the text. Remember, when drawing conclusions, be sure to use pieces of information found in the passage to support your choices.

As the sun found its way through the sheer curtains covering the rustic cabin windows, the excited boys made their way to the breakfast table. The boys had great anticipation of what the day would hold for them.

Near the door to the cabin stood three well-used fishing rods, nets, and hip boots. The bait was to be picked up fresh in the morning on their way to the lake.

Within a short time of waking, the three sat down at the table and devoured the hearty breakfast of sausage, pancakes, hot chocolate, and fresh fruit. It had been some time since the boys enjoyed a homemade breakfast prepared by their dad. The boys' enthusiasm for this trip was evident from the moment dad had sprung the idea on them back in late February.

As the fresh air of early April permeated the country scene, all were eager to get started, and so they quickly dressed, grabbed their gear, and were on their way to the lake.

On the walk to the lake, the boys and their dad noted the beauty of the countryside. Wildflowers dotted the roadside, and the fresh blades of newborn grass found their way to the surface of the moist and fertile soil.

Within a short span of time, the three arrived by the dock they had come to know so well over the past ten years. Although the dock had weathered, it still held the memories of many well-fought battles with fish that refused to succumb easily.

The day's fishing had yielded few fish for the threesome, but the day had been filled with much conversation. This was the kind of conversation that dads and sons remember for a lifetime.

2-26A. Continued

1. Which excerpt presented in the passage allows you to conclude that this would be an experience the boys would tell their own sons about some day?
   A. On the walk to the lake, the boys and their dad noted the beauty of the countryside.
   B. Within a short span of time, the three arrived by the dock they had come to know so well over the past ten years.
   C. This was the kind of conversation that dads and sons remember for a lifetime.
   D. As the fresh air of early April permeated the country scene, all were eager to get started, and so they quickly dressed, grabbed their gear, and were on their way to the lake.

2. We can conclude that the boys value this experience with their dad based upon which of these excerpts?
   A. Near the door to the cabin stood three well-used fishing rods, nets, and hip boots.
   B. On the walk to the lake, the boys and their dad noted the beauty of the countryside.
   C. The boys' enthusiasm for this trip was evident from the moment dad had sprung the idea on them back in late February.
   D. Within a short time of waking, the three sat down at the table and devoured the hearty breakfast of sausage, pancakes, hot chocolate, and fresh fruit.

3. Which excerpt from the passage leads you to conclude that this trip is taken with some regularity?
   A. The boys had great anticipation of what the day would hold for them.
   B. On the walk to the lake, the boys and their dad noted the beauty of the countryside.
   C. Within a short span of time, the three arrived by the dock they had come to know so well over the past ten years.
   D. The day's fishing had yielded few fish for the threesome, but the day had been filled with much conversation.

4. Which excerpt from the passage helps you conclude that the daily routines on this trip are different from those during the rest of the year?
   A. The boys had great anticipation of what the day would hold for them.
   B. It had been some time since the boys enjoyed a homemade breakfast prepared by their dad.
   C. Although the dock had weathered, it still held the memories of many well-fought battles with fish that refused to succumb easily.
   D. Wildflowers dotted the roadside, and the fresh blades of newborn grass found their way to the surface of the moist and fertile soil.

5. Of the following excerpts, which one does not help you conclude that the boys and their father enjoyed their fishing experiences?
   A. The boys had great anticipation of what the day would hold for them.
   B. As the fresh air of early April permeated the country scene, all were eager to get started, and so they quickly dressed, grabbed their gear, and were on their way to the lake.
   C. The boys' enthusiasm for this trip was evident from the moment dad had sprung the idea on them back in late February.
   D. Near the door to the cabin stood three well-used fishing rods, nets, and hip boots.

2-27. ANOTHER STRATEGY FOR DRAWING CONCLUSIONS

As you read a story or other kinds of text, the author will present ideas. To be an effective reader, you must be able to read the information presented and piece the information together in order to draw conclusions. In standardized tests you are often presented with a written passage and asked to draw conclusions by combining pieces of information found in the passage.

TESTING TIP:

One strategy for drawing conclusions is to read the test questions first. Then read through the passage looking for specific information that can help you draw a conclusion.

Name_____ Date_____

2-27A. DRAWING CONCLUSIONS

Activity: Read the passage below. Then consider the questions that follow and select the best answer based upon the information found in the text. Remember, when drawing conclusions, be sure to use pieces of information found in the passage to support your choices.

Bill, Ashley, Marcos, and Harry had planned this bicycle hike for several weeks. They had spent many weeks preparing their bikes and polishing them for this fifteen-mile hike through the mountains not far from their community.

The day had finally arrived, the weather was perfect, and the preparations were all complete. With backpacks in place, the four set off for the day's adventure. As the four began, Marcos's first attempts at pedaling were rough and irregular but within minutes the pedaling smoothed out. At no point were his friends aware of his difficulty. The four were off and took in the fresh country air and beautiful scenes of wildflowers and the early spring grasses.

"What a grand day we have!" exclaimed Ashley.

"You bet, we couldn't have asked for a finer day," Harry echoed.

As the foursome approached the rise to the first mountain, each geared up for the effort that would be required of them. At this point, Marcos had slipped back, once again experiencing a rather choppy pedaling sequence. As happened earlier in the ride, he worked it through and caught up with the group.

Soon they were approaching the steep dirt trail that would take them winding through the rocky wooded terrain. Bill led the group with Ashley, Harry, and Marcos behind. As they rounded the first bend, the trail became steeper and they picked up speed. The distance between riders lengthened. Marcos hit a tree root that crossed the trail, sending him careening into the side of the brush. In a matter of seconds, the other three were out of sight and earshot.

As Marcos assessed the damage, he realized he was only bruised, but the bike had a broken chain. Deserted in the wooded undergrowth, his options were few. There were no cars, houses, telephones or other bikers who could help him repair his bike. It might be a long time before his friends realized his absence.

Pulling out the trail map, Marcos was happy to see that the trail looped around, enabling him to catch up with his friends through a short cut if he hurried. Running at a fast clip, Marcos raced through the undergrowth on foot in an effort to find his fellow bikers.

With no markers or obvious signs pointing to the right direction, Marcos checked the map and hoped for the best as he hurried in pursuit of his friends. While en route, he encountered a stream moving quite swiftly that challenged his ingenuity to cross.

Marcos took advantage of nearby rocks and fallen trees and placed them strategically across the waterway, allowing him safe passage.

As he made his way across the stream, he saw a clearing in the woods. Following this lead, he emerged back on the trail and met up with his friends who were still unaware of his absence.

2-27A. Continued

1. Which excerpt from the passage helps you conclude that Marcos was resourceful?

   A. As Marcos assessed the damage, he realized he was only bruised, but the bike had a broken chain.

   B. Marcos hit a tree root that crossed the trail, sending him careening into the side of the brush.

   C. Following this lead, he emerged back on the trail and met up with his friends who were still unaware of his absence.

   D. Marcos took advantage of nearby rocks and fallen trees and placed them strategically across the waterway, allowing him safe passage.

2. Which excerpt from the passage helps you conclude that Marcos's friends had not planned for safety checks during the bike ride?

   A. Bill, Ashley, Marcos, and Harry had planned this bicycle hike for several weeks now.

   B. Following this lead, he emerged back on the trail and met up with his friends who were still unaware of his absence.

   C. As Marcos assessed the damage, he realized he was only bruised, but the bike had a broken chain.

   D. They had spent many weeks preparing their bikes and polishing them for this fifteen-mile hike through the mountains not far from their community.

3. Which excerpt from the passage helps you conclude that this bike trip might have taken place in the Northeast part of the United States?

   A. The four were off and took in the fresh country air and beautiful scenes of wildflowers and the early spring grasses.

   B. Soon they were approaching the steep dirt trail that would take them winding through the rocky wooded terrain.

   C. There were no cars, houses, telephones or other bikers who could help him repair his bike.

   D. While en route, he encountered a stream moving quite swiftly that challenged his ingenuity to cross.

4. Which excerpt from the passage helps you conclude that Marcos knew the other three bikers before the day of the trip?

   A. Bill led the group with Ashley, Harry, and Marcos behind.

   B. Running at a fast clip, Marcos raced through the undergrowth on foot in an effort to find his fellow bikers.

   C. With backpacks in place, the four set off for the day's adventure.

   D. Bill, Ashley, Marcos, and Harry had planned this bicycle hike for several weeks now.

5. Which excerpt from the passage helps you conclude that Marcos used effective problem-solving skills?

   A. Marcos hit a tree root that crossed the trail, sending him careening into the side of the brush.

   B. As Marcos assessed the damage, he realized he was only bruised, but the bike had a broken chain.

   C. Pulling out the trail map, Marcos was happy to see that the trail looped around, enabling him to catch up with his friends through a short cut if he hurried.

   D. As the four began, Marcos's first attempts at pedaling were rough and irregular but within minutes the pedaling smoothed out.

2-28. A STRATEGY FOR RECOGNIZING AUTHOR'S STYLE

As you read a story or other kinds of text, the author's attitude, purpose, or tone is often evident. The author's *attitude* is his or her point of view. The author's *purpose* is why he or she wrote the piece, what he or she is trying to convince the reader to believe. *Tone* refers to the manner in which the author writes. Tone may be sympathetic, sarcastic, humorous, or formal. To be an effective reader, you must be able to read the information presented and interpret the author's perspective. In standardized tests you are often presented with a written passage and asked to identify the author's attitude, purpose, or tone.

TESTING TIP:

One strategy for recognizing author's style is to read the test question and the possible answers. Then read through the passage looking for specific words and/or phrases that would help you to determine the author's attitude, purpose, or tone.

2-28A. RECOGNIZING AUTHOR'S STYLE

Activity: Read the passage below. Then consider the questions that follow and select the best answer based upon the information found in the text.

Television is the leading reason why American children perform so poorly in school and on standardized tests. Viewing television shows requires no thinking or creative processes on the part of the child. It encourages a passive response from the viewers and does little to challenge or stimulate the brain.

Much of the material presented in sitcoms, talk shows, and cartoons is often inappropriate and used to shock the viewer. This, of course, helps to maintain the viewer's interest but often results in an attitude of acceptance of inappropriate behavior.

Unsupervised television viewing prevents children from developing their minds and bodies. American children are not taking to the playgrounds as they have in the past. This must stop! No longer can America tolerate the amount of time our youth spend in front of the television screen. Action must be taken now!

2-28A. Continued

1. Which of the following best describes the author's tone when speaking about sitcoms?
   A. Humorous
   B. Sympathetic
   C. Angry
   D. Patient

2. Which of the following best describes the author's attitude when speaking about children's television viewing habits?
   A. Television viewing leads to educational success.
   B. Television viewing is detrimental to the full development of both mind and body.
   C. Television viewing encourages snacking.
   D. Television viewing promotes good citizenship.

3. Which of the following best describes the author's purpose in writing this passage?
   A. To encourage more television viewing on the weekends
   B. To convince children to turn off their televisions in favor of more active play and study
   C. To lead a protest demonstration in Washington, D.C. against television viewing
   D. To show his or her love of the nature shows and news commentaries on television

Directions: Using quotations from the passage, find evidence to support your answers to numbers 1 through 3. Write each quotation in the space provided below.

4. Question 1: _____

_____

5. Question 2: _____

_____

6. Question 3: _____

_____

Extension: Use a newspaper editorial to identify the author's purpose, tone, and attitude toward the subject discussed. Find evidence to support your responses.

SECTION THREE

Language

SPELLING

MECHANICS AND USAGE

SPELLING

Standardized and classroom tests often use similar vocabulary when presenting test questions and directions. Familiarity with these words and phrasings can be helpful when taking such tests. Increased understanding of these words and phrases will help you in responding to such test questions.

Here are some of the common directions used on standardized tests for testing spelling:

- Find the misspelled word.
- Which of the following sentences contains a spelling error?

3-1. A STRATEGY FOR PROOFREADING TO FIND ERRORS

When composing a written piece of work, it is important that you follow the conventions of correct spelling. On a standardized test, you are sometimes called upon to identify spelling errors. Sometimes these errors are within single sentences, and you are asked to choose the sentence containing a spelling error.

Example: Which of the following sentences contains a spelling error?

A.   The day's outing took the students into the woodland forest.
B.   The forest floor was covered with firns and mosses.
C.   Birds sang, squirrels scampered, and the deer watched alertly.
D.   The canopy of leaves filtered sunlight and protected the creatures.

Explanation: The correct choice here is sentence B since the word *firns* should be spelled *ferns.*

TESTING TIP:

Read each sentence carefully, placing your finger under each word as you analyze its spelling. Go slowly, noticing words that you suspect may be misspelled.

3-1A. PROOFREADING TO FIND ERRORS

Activity: Read each set of sentences. Choose the sentence in each group containing the spelling error.

1. A. It was the perfect day for the annual track meet.
    B. All of the contestants were gathered on the track for the opening ceremony.
    C. On signal the marching band played the national anthem.
    D. Once the rendition was complete, the crowds cheered the start of the events.

2. A. Picnics are popular weekend events during the summer.
    B. The parks in our area are filled with many picnickers.
    C. Besides the wonderful foods that are eaten, there are many games of volleyball and horseshoes.
    D. Memorial Day, July Forth, and Labor Day are popular days for picnics.

3. A. New England is a popular site for fall tourists.
    B. The crisp air and colorful fall foliage is quite an attracshun.
    C. The New England cities offer many fine recreational opportunities.
    D. This region of our country is quite scenic.

4. A. Public libraries are filled with many kinds of reading material.
    B. Of course, the reference section offers encyclopedias and dictionaries.
    C. The nonfiction section offers many informative books.
    D. The fiction section has a wide variety of stories avalable.

5. A. Earth is characterized by both land and water formations.
    B. The majority of the earth's surface is covered by water.
    C. The major land masses are called continents.
    D. The continents themselfs feature a wide variety of geographic land formations.

6. A. Americans enjoy many modern-day conveniences.
    B. Computers have become quite sophisticated and offer the public many new services.
    C. Mobile telephones permit one to talk on the phone from almost anywhere at all.
    D. Laser tecknology has enabled the medical field to perform new kinds of surgery.

7. A. Shopping for a new car can be a trying experience.
    B. First, you must know the features you want in your car.
    C. Second, you must know your preferences regarding the car's styling.
    D. With this information you can begin the process of making your car purchase.

3-1A. Continued

8. A. The movies are a popular form of entertainment.
   B. Some prefur the children's movies.
   C. Others like the thrill of the action adventures.
   D. Still others prefer a romantic storyline filmed in a beautiful location.

9. A. Riding a bicycle at night can be a hazardous experience.
   B. Night riders must have a light on the bicycle so they are visible to other traffic.
   C. Reflective clothing items should be worn to increase visibility.
   D. Riding only in those areas designated for bikes is also recomended.

10. A. Deserts are very interesting habitats.
    B. The various forms of cactus always intreeg visitors to the desert.
    C. The unique creatures native to the desert regions are also rather incredible.
    D. Of course, the extreme climatic conditions of the desert areas are responsible for the life forms found there.

3-1B. PROOFREADING TO FIND ERRORS

Activity: Read each set of sentences. Choose the sentence in each group containing the spelling error.

1. A. The fall foliage had already begun to turn to the attractive colors of yellow, orange, and red.
   B. A strole through the woods on Saturday was most enjoyable.
   C. The wildlife in the wooded setting was noticeably quiet.
   D. Visitors from the city enjoyed the full day of activity.

2. A. This season the hurricanes were frequent and serious.
   B. Hurricane Eduardo prompted many travelers to leave for home earlier then expected.
   C. Radios were the primary source of news for those remaining on the island.
   D. No serious injuries were reported.

3. A. A bicycle ride on a crisp fall morning makes for healthy exercise.
   B. The river was choppy for the morning.
   C. Several small vessils could be seen docked near the pier.
   D. Flags were flying high in the marina.

4. A. Our neighborhood parks are busy on Sunday mornings.
   B. Call ahead if you intend to picnic.
   C. A variety of challenging phisical activities awaits you at the park nearest you.
   D. Park rangers ensure that the park is a safe place for the people.

5. A. Farm work is exausting.
   B. Preparing the fields for planting takes much effort.
   C. Modern technology assists the farmer today.
   D. A warm climate aids in the growing of many popular crops.

6. A. There are many new forms of recreation available today.
   B. Roller blading has quickly become one of the more popular forms of exercise.
   C. Many youngsters today begin to ski at the early ages of five and six.
   D. Running is also commen among the physically fit generation.

7. A. Many new television channels are available through cable.
   B. Favorite shows seem to be on Monday evenings.
   C. Vote for your favorite television situation comedy.
   D. Were you awar of the new sauces?

3-1B. Continued

8. A. Music education is important for all youth.
   B. A visit to Lincoln Center in New York is a must for all to see.
   C. The acoustics in the main concert hall are wonderfull.
   D. Musical scores often make the difference in the success of a song.

9. A. The traffic on local roads has resently increased.
   B. Police patrols are up in order to address this problem.
   C. Bicycle riders are encouraged to stay off these roads.
   D. Parents are encouraged to train their children to follow the rules of the road when riding a bicycle.

10. A. Spectator sports seem to attract more and more fans.
    B. A college football game can easily be sold out for a Saturday game by Thursday.
    C. Sports is a big bisness.
    D. Season ticket holders should also have parking permits.

3-2. A STRATEGY FOR PROOFREADING TO FIND HOMONYM ERRORS

When composing a written piece of work, it is important that you follow the conventions of correct spelling. On a standardized test, you are sometimes called upon to identify spelling errors. Sometimes these errors are within single sentences, and you are asked to choose the sentence containing a spelling error. Homonyms, words that sound alike but are spelled differently, are often misspelled in writing. Be sure to focus your attention on these words as you analyze a set of sentences for misspelled words.

Example: Which of the following sentences contains a spelling error?
A. The woman was directed to park the car over there.
B. Unfortunately, her car wouldn't fit in the space.
C. The parking attendants said their spaces were standard size.
D. "Their all the same!" shouted the attendant.

Explanation: The correct choice here is sentence D since the word *Their* should be spelled *They're*. *They're* is the contraction for *They are,* and that wording correctly fits this sentence.

TESTING TIP:

Read each sentence carefully, placing your finger under each word as you analyze its spelling. Go slowly, noticing words that are suspect.

3-2A. PROOFREADING TO FIND HOMONYM ERRORS

Activity: Read each set of sentences. Choose the sentence in each group containing the spelling error.

1. A. When the guests arrive here in our country, we will show them the many sights.
    B. Were you able to hear what I said?
    C. The visitors traveled from hear to there.
    D. Would you please pick up that chair and bring it over here?

2. A. The students will meat their counselors early in September.
    B. An old-fashioned restaurant offers an array of fine meats for the guests.
    C. Those attending the track meet will be excused at 2:00 P.M.
    D. Please select your entree from the following cuts of meat.

3. A. Where did the landscapers put the tools?
    B. Because of the extreme heat, please be sure to wear comfortable clothing.
    C. Did you hear where the next performance will be held?
    D. If you drive on the bad tire much more, it is sure to where out.

4. A. After working for four hours, you may take a brake.
    B. The swift runner is sure to break the school record.
    C. Her bicycle is at the shop because the brake pedal is not working properly.
    D. If you are not careful, the vase may break.

5. A. Although the ship has expensive technology on board, it still went off course.
    B. The coarse texture of the fabric made it uncomfortable.
    C. Which of the two courses do you intend to drop from your schedule?
    D. Given the problem before you, which coarse of action do you intend to take?

6. A. When asked what she wanted, she responded, "I'll take a large piece of cake."
    B. Which piece of the pie is yours?
    C. The United Nations is an international organization concerned with world peace.
    D. Several peaces of the puzzle were missing from the package.

7. A. Although the country exports many products, its principle export is lumber.
    B. Because of the severe weather, the principal announced the shortened day's schedule.
    C. Our country was founded on a number of basic humanitarian principles.
    D. One's principles are his or her important beliefs.

3-2A. Continued

8. A. The pitcher threw a perfect no hitter on Saturday night.
   B. Through the narrow inlet the captain guided the ship.
   C. She used a brand new and colorful pitcher when serving the iced tea.
   D. A number of the hikers traveled threw the narrow passage.

9. A. Five of the problems proved to difficult to solve.
   B. I, too, was having difficulty with solving the problem.
   C. Two of the guests complained of the lack of heat in the cabin.
   D. If you walk to the left, you will see what I mean.

10. A. I placed my gift for you're sister on the table.
    B. Your address will change effective August 1.
    C. Of all of the relatives attending, you're my favorite.
    D. Twelve of your friends were invited to the event.

3-3. A STRATEGY FOR PROOFREADING TO FIND THE ERROR

When composing a written piece of work, it is important that you follow the conventions of correct spelling. On a standardized test, you are sometimes called upon to identify spelling errors. Sometimes these errors are included within a written passage, and you are asked to choose the misspelled word. There is often a last choice of *No Error*. Choose this answer when no spelling error appears.

Example: Choose the letter of the spelling error or the *No Error* response in each selection.

1.   Harry (A) eagerly anticipated his (B) birthday. He (C) couldn't wait for his (D) freinds to come for pizza and a sleep over.

Explanation: The correct choice here is D since the word *freinds* should be spelled *friends*.

TESTING TIP:

Read each passage carefully, placing your finger under each word as you analyze its spelling. Go slowly, noticing words that are suspect.

3-3A. PROOFREADING TO FIND THE ERROR

Activity: Read each passage. Choose the misspelled word in each passage. If there is no error, select the *No Error* response instead.

1. While (A) walking through the (B) isle, the woman (C) noticed the competitive pricing of the products.

   A
   B
   C
   D. No Error

2. She (A) anticipated that there would be many (B) frightened children since the (C) fireworks display is usually both bright and loud.

   A
   B
   C
   D. No Error

3. A shopping (A) complex of more (B) then one hundred stores opened (C) recently in our community.

   A
   B
   C
   D. No Error

4. (A) According to the surveys completed by our (B) customers, Sally Sue Wright is the most (C) corteous employee working in our shop.

   A
   B
   C
   D. No Error

5. When (A) rehearsing for the (B) performance, an actor would (C) embarass easily when forgetting a line.

   A
   B
   C
   D. No Error

6. Once you have earned the (A) privilege to drive a car, you must use good (B) judgement to avoid injury to both you and your (C) passengers.

   A
   B
   C
   D. No Error

3-3A. Continued

7. Younger (A) sibblings can be (B) challenging to (C) supervise, especially if they are under four years old.

    A

    B

    C

    D. No Error

8. It is usually (A) sufficient to wait for two weeks following an (B) appliance (C) installation to be sure that it is working correctly.

    A

    B

    C

    D. No Error

9. In my (A) experience travel to (B) foreign countries is very (C) educational.

    A

    B

    C

    D. No Error

10. All of the movies we've seen (A) recently featured a (B) villainous main (C) character.

    A

    B

    C

    D. No Error

3-3B. PROOFREADING TO FIND THE ERROR

Activity: Read each passage. Choose the misspelled word in each passage. If there is no error, select the *No Error* response instead.

1. (A) Efforts were made to (B) maintain a dry baseball (C) feild.

    A

    B

    C

    D. No Error

2. She left for the (A) carnival (B) earlier than we had (C) exspected.

    A

    B

    C

    D. No Error

3. Our (A) country is rich in natural (B) recourses and fine minds ready to (C) develop them.

    A

    B

    C

    D. No Error

4. (A) Who's idea was it to create a (B) modernized assembly line (C) system?

    A

    B

    C

    D. No Error

5. The newest (A) furnichur line that we carry is from North Carolina, a well-known (B) factory outlet (C) center.

    A

    B

    C

    D. No Error

6. Once the (A) commuter train pulls into the (B) station area, the engines of the waiting cars begin to (C) roar.

    A

    B

    C

    D. No Error

3-3B. *Continued*

7. As we (A) hiked into the (B) medow area, we observed many rare (C) species of butterflies.

   A

   B

   C

   D. No Error

8. (A) Chefs at three area (B) renowned restaurants were on the noon (C) news.

   A

   B

   C

   D. No Error

9. For those who travel to Hawaii, (A) island hopping is a popular (B) toorist (C) activity.

   A

   B

   C

   D. No Error

10. (A) Holiday shopping (B) proved to be (C) veiry enjoyable for Katherine.

   A

   B

   C

   D. No Error

3-4. ANOTHER STRATEGY FOR PROOFREADING TO FIND THE ERROR

On a standardized or classroom test, you are sometimes called upon to identify the misspelled word from a list of possible choices. Often there is a pattern common to the words. Examine the words carefully in order to determine the misspelled word. If no spelling error exists, choose the *No Error* response.

Example: 1.   A.   neighbors
                      B.   reciept
                      C.   weight
                      D.   No error

Explanation: The correct choice here is B since the word *reciept* is misspelled. It should be spelled *receipt*. Notice that the *ie* spelling rule is being tested here.

TESTING TIP:

Analyze each word carefully, placing your finger under each word as you examine its spelling. Go slowly as you look for the misspelled word.

Name_____ Date_____

3-4A. PROOFREADING TO FIND THE ERROR

Activity: Choose the misspelled word in each list.

1. A. illegal
    B. ilegible
    C. illogical
    D. No Error

2. A. lovelyness
    B. cried
    C. burial
    D. No Error

3. A. radios
    B. patios
    C. tomatoes
    D. No Error

4. A. brothers-in-law
    B. mothers-in-law
    C. fathers-in-laws
    D. No Error

5. A. deer
    B. sheeps
    C. mouse
    D. No Error

6. A. truly
    B. argument
    C. judgement
    D. No Error

7. A. comeing
    B. lovable
    C. hoping
    D. No Error

8. A. traveler
    B. canceled
    C. stencilling
    D. No Error

9. A. thieves
    B. beliefs
    C. shelfs
    D. No Error

10. A. gooses
    B. oxen
    C. teeth
    D. No Error

3-4B. PROOFREADING TO FIND THE ERROR

Activity: Choose the misspelled word in each list.

1. A. honesty
    B. ohnest
    C. honest
    D. No Error

2. A. hassle
    B. hustle
    C. hussle
    D. No Error

3. A. completely
    B. thoroughly
    C. earnest
    D. No Error

4. A. simulated
    B. syncapation
    C. actually
    D. No Error

5. A. lease
    B. rental
    C. purchess
    D. No Error

6. A. forword
    B. preface
    C. prior
    D. No Error

7. A. raceing
    B. diving
    C. ascending
    D. No Error

8. A. computer
    B. favorite
    C. stupendous
    D. No Error

9. A. mannerly
    B. subtly
    C. overtly
    D. No Error

10. A. calculater
    B. calculator
    C. calculators
    D. No Error

3-5. A STRATEGY FOR RECOGNIZING CORRECT SPELLING

On a standardized or classroom test, you are sometimes called upon to identify the correctly spelled word from a list of possible choices. The word is spelled in a variety of ways, only one of which is correct. Since the words are nearly the same in appearance, it is important that you carefully analyze the spelling letter by letter. A sentence is often provided to give context for the word.

Example: Andy had a remarkable _____ while whale watching.
         A. experence
         B. expearience
         C. experience
         D. expereince

Explanation: The correct choice here is C since the word *experience* is correctly spelled.

TESTING TIP:

Analyze each word carefully, placing your finger under each word as you examine its spelling. Go slowly as you look for the correctly spelled word.

3-5A. RECOGNIZING CORRECT SPELLING

Activity: Read each sentence in order to determine the context of the word. Choose the correctly spelled word in each list.

1. An uproar of laughter came from the theater as the _____ entertainer performed.
   - A. humerous
   - B. hoomerous
   - C. humorous
   - D. humarous

2. Of the many kinds of books on the market, _____ are my favorite.
   - A. misteries
   - B. misterys
   - C. mysteries
   - D. mysterys

3. As Lindsay came into the house, she recognized her lost puppy _____.
   - A. immediatly
   - B. imediately
   - C. immediately
   - D. immediatley

4. Although hours had passed, he remained very _____.
   - A. pashent
   - B. patent
   - C. pashient
   - D. patient

5. In order to _____ success, you must study hard and work long hours.
   - A. acheeve
   - B. achieve
   - C. acheive
   - D. achieev

6. The party was _____ scheduled for Saturday, but the date was changed.
   - A. orignally
   - B. originaly
   - C. originaley
   - D. originally

3-5A. Continued

7. Because he had practiced so long and still did not win the event, he was overwhelmed with _____.
   A. disapointment
   B. disappointmant
   C. disappointment
   D. dissapointment

8. As a result of the fingerprints found at the crime scene, the neighbors were _____ of the local suspect.
   A. suspishous
   B. suspicious
   C. suspicous
   D. suspishious

9. Once the curtains opened, the audience was able to identify the star _____.
   A. immediatly
   B. imediately
   C. immedietly
   D. immediately

10. A washing machine has many _____ parts, and occasionally the machine may need to be serviced.
    A. mechanical
    B. mechanikal
    C. mechaincal
    D. meckanical

3-5B. RECOGNIZING CORRECT SPELLING

Activity: Read each sentence in order to determine the context of the word. Choose the correctly spelled word in each list.

1. The sandwich was one of the best I had ever _____.
   A. devowered
   B. devowert
   C. devouret
   D. devoured

2. Mustard and relish _____ to the taste.
   A. contribut
   B. contributte
   C. contriboot
   D. contribute

3. The picnic basket was filled to the brim with _____ foods.
   A. delishus
   B. delishious
   C. delicious
   D. dilicioush

4. Today's supermarkets stock _____ food products.
   A. unuzual
   B. unusual
   C. unushul
   D. unusuhal

5. Fresh fruit and vegetables are beautifully _____.
   A. desplayed
   B. displaed
   C. displaid
   D. displayed

6. Many food stores have their own bakeries ready to serve the _____.
   A. customer
   B. customor
   C. customir
   D. customur

3-5B. *Continued*

7. Frozen dinners are popular among the hardworking _____.
   A. bussinespeople
   B. buzinesspeople
   C. businespeople
   D. businesspeople

8. Take-out foods account for a large _____ of the food consumed today.
   A. porshon
   B. portion
   C. porshen
   D. porshin

9. Restaurant menus have become far more _____.
   A. colerful
   B. colerfull
   C. colorful
   D. colerfel

10. The picnic offered many wonderful _____.
    A. activeties
    B. activities
    C. activitiese
    D. activitis

MECHANICS AND USAGE

Standardized and classroom tests often use similar vocabulary when presenting test questions and directions. Familiarity with these words and phrasings can be helpful when taking such tests. Increased understanding of these words and phrases will help you in responding to such test questions.

Here are some common directions used on tests for testing mechanics and usage:

- What kind of letter is this? What are the parts of the letter called?
- Which of the following sentences has a capitalization error?
- Which of the following sentences has a punctuation error?
- Which of the following sentences contains a usage error?
- In the following outline, what letter or number belongs in the blank?
- Which of the following is not a run-on sentence?
- Which of the following sentences contains a grammatical error?
- In which line should a comma be changed to a colon?
- Which of the following is the correct way to indicate the title of a book within a sentence?
- Which of the following sentences demonstrates the correct (incorrect) use of quotation marks?
- Which of the following sentences is capitalized correctly?
- What is the best punctuation mark to put in the blank?

3-6. A STRATEGY FOR IDENTIFYING CAPITALIZATION ERRORS

On a standardized or classroom test, you are sometimes called upon to identify errors in capitalization.

Example: 1.   Which of the following sentences contains a capitalization error?
A.   He received an order from commander Anderson.
B.   Private Billings was scheduled to go to the testing site.
C.   His new assignment required him to work with the general.
D.   At this time, General White was pleased to work with Private Billings.

Explanation: The correct choice here is A since the word *commander* should be capitalized as it is a title used with the name.

TESTING TIP:

Remember that proper names, the first word in a sentence, the first word in a quotation, and important words from titles should all be capitalized.

3-6A. IDENTIFYING CAPITALIZATION ERRORS

Activity: Choose the sentence in each set containing the capitalization error.

1. _____

   A. Last summer, we visited the Grand Canyon in Arizona.
   B. Then we drove to Yosemite National Park and Bryce Canyon.
   C. Even though our trip was in august, we had a light snowfall in Yosemite.
   D. We ended our trip in San Francisco with a visit to Alcatraz.

2. _____

   A. When I was seven, my best friend was Jeff, my neighbor.
   B. as I grew, I developed more good friends, including Sam, Adam, and Rosa.
   C. In junior high, I became inseparable with Todd, but did lots of things with a large group of friends.
   D. Now I find I want to spend all my time with Amy.

3. _____

   A. Volcanoes are one of the most interesting and exciting natural wonders.
   B. When Mt. Vesuvius erupted in 79 A.D., it buried the city of Pompeii in Ancient Rome.
   C. Mount St. Helens scattered dust and ash throughout Washington and oregon.
   D. The eruption of Krakatoa, which blew away most of the island in the Pacific Ocean, was the largest eruption on record.

4. _____

   A. My birthday is august 31, which makes me one of the youngest in my grade at school.
   B. When I entered kindergarten at the Maple Street School, Mrs. Jones was my teacher.
   C. At that time, we lived at 161 Grove Street, Maplewood, Ohio.
   D. We moved to Cleveland when I was in sixth grade.

5. _____

   A. This year I have english, French, and Science in the morning.
   B. My teachers are Mr. Layton, Mrs. Dey, and Dr. Washington.
   C. Our class trip will be to New York City where we will visit the Statue of Liberty and the United Nations.
   D. An ambassador from the Far East will give us a special tour of the UN.

6. _____

   A. "Where are you going?" Matthew asked.
   B. Sam answered, "i'm on my way to buy new soccer shoes."
   C. They went to The Soccer Store, the new shop in the mall.
   D. Matthew bought a pair of Umbro shorts, too.

3-6A. Continued

7. _____

    A. Next Monday will be halloween, October 31.
    B. The Ritz Hotel and the Bailey Theater are both on Lee Street.
    C. John O'Hara still has a slight Irish accent.
    D. My favorite museum is the National Air and Space Museum in Washington.

8. _____

    A. For my summer reading, I finished *The Count of Monte Cristo*.
    B. Captain ahab was the main character in *Moby Dick*.
    C. I always read the editorials in *The New York Times*.
    D. My favorite book is *A Tale of Two Cities* by Charles Dickens.

9. _____

    A. Sara's new puppy is an english setter.
    B. Aunt Joan, Uncle Bob, and Grandmother Miller will come to dinner.
    C. My grandmother is almost sixty years old.
    D. Last May, my little sister graduated from Williams College.

10. _____

    A. The rocky mountains provide a variety of outdoor experiences for visitors.
    B. To find the library, go north two blocks and then west two blocks.
    C. Sally Summers jogs along a three-mile route through the middle of Pottersville every morning.
    D. The Deaner Company manufactures rubber bands.

3-7. A STRATEGY FOR IDENTIFYING CORRECT CAPITALIZATION

On a standardized or classroom test, you are sometimes called upon to identify the correct use of capitalization. You may be given a list of sentences in which only one sentence is correctly capitalized.

Example: 1.   Which of the following sentences is capitalized correctly?
            A.   "Have you visited the grand Canyon?" asked Meg.
            B.   "No, i haven't," responded Kerry.
            C.   "it's great! You should go."
            D.   "I'll think about it."

Explanation: The correct choice here is D since all words contained are capitalized appropriately.

TESTING TIP:

Remember that proper names, the first word in a sentence, the first word in a quotation, and important words from titles should all be capitalized.

146

3-7A. IDENTIFYING CORRECT CAPITALIZATION

Activity: Choose the sentence in each set that is correctly capitalized.

1. _____
   A. I was born in Summit, New Jersey, but spent my childhood in Basking Ridge.
   B. I attended Happy Time Nursery School, Woodrow Wilson Elementary School, and Grimes middle School.
   C. My family moved to Tampa, Florida and then to san Francisco, California.
   D. On the fourth of July, we saw fireworks and a town parade.

2. _____
   A. David Chang was born in Peking, but now lives in santa Fe, New Mexico.
   B. The development of civilization in ancient Egypt depended upon the yearly flooding of the Nile river.
   C. The League of Women Voters meets every month at the Civic Center on First Street.
   D. Albert Einstein was a familiar figure at Princeton university.

3. _____
   A. Olympic National Park has no relationship to the Special Olympics held each summer.
   B. I am taking a history class that covers the Revolutionary war, the Civil war, and the Vietnam war.
   C. October 31 is better known to children as halloween.
   D. Visiting the Vietnam memorial in Washington, D.C. is a very moving experience.

4. _____
   A. My grade in science went up this marking period.
   B. The environmental club visited the smithsonian this fall.
   C. Springfield high school held closing exercises on June 4 last year.
   D. I read a historical novel set in Britain during world war II.

5. _____
   A. Senator Wright voted against the recommendations of the Senate finance committee.
   B. The Elephant's Ear is my favorite restaurant in New York City.
   C. The Ritz theater is next to Marigold's Dry Cleaners on South Street.
   D. During my Summer vacation, I visited Bermuda where I swam, rode a motor bike, and played tennis.

6. _____
   A. Many students do not know that Samuel Clemens and mark twain are the same person.
   B. *Tom Sawyer* and *Huckleberry Finn* are my favorite books by Mark Twain.
   C. Injun joe is a frightening character who lives up to his reputation in these novels set in the south.
   D. Tom always manages to outwit aunt Polly in order to escape her chores and have fun.

3-7A. Continued

7. _____
    A. Saturn is a planet named after the roman God of Farming.
    B. The thousands of rings around Saturn are made up of ice, dust, and rock.
    C. The rings are held in place by the Gravity of Saturn.
    D. More than twenty Moons have been discovered orbiting Saturn.

8. _____
    A. In North America, the Rockies are the largest mountain chain.
    B. The highest mountain is Mount Everest in the himalayas of Asia.
    C. Many mountains were formed by Volcanoes.
    D. Some mountains, like those in the Swiss Alps, are known for their Ski Resorts.

9. _____
    A. My english teacher, Mr. David Price, is actually from Liverpool, England.
    B. My science teacher, Mrs. Toni Brescher, has us work in the science lab at least twice a week.
    C. Rockford High School won the state championship in soccer last Fall.
    D. Our new principal, Ms. Johnson, began teaching one spanish class in order to help her learn about our school.

10. _____
    A. The space shuttle challenger was launched from Cape Canaveral.
    B. One of my best friends moved to Cleveland, Ohio to attend Smith School.
    C. Giants Stadium, in East Rutherford, is the Home Stadium for both the Giants and the Jets.
    D. Babe Ruth is probably the most famous Baseball player of all time.

3-8. A STRATEGY FOR IDENTIFYING PUNCTUATION ERRORS

On a standardized or classroom test, you are sometimes called upon to identify errors in punctuation. In this activity, you will focus specifically on the use of end marks and commas.

Example: 1.   Which of the following sentences contains a punctuation error?
A.   The tadpoles were growing, and would soon be ready to leap onto land.
B.   They were still eating algae in the pond water, but they would become fierce hunters of insects in a few weeks.
C.   As their legs grew stronger, their tails shortened.
D.   Camouflage would help the frogs locate and catch food as well as protect them from enemies.

Explanation: The correct choice here is A since a comma is not needed. A comma would be needed only if both sides of the sentence expressed a complete thought.

TESTING TIP:

Remember to use commas correctly in a series, in compound and complex sentences, in phrases and clauses, in words of direct address, and in dates and addresses. Review the rules if necessary.

3-8A. IDENTIFYING PUNCTUATION ERRORS

Activity: Choose the sentence in each set that contains a punctuation error.

1. _____
   A. Mary asked how much the puppy cost?
   B. The salesman replied, "$75.00 for the beagle."
   C. Mary had saved up $54, but that wasn't enough.
   D. Happily, her mother loaned her the rest of the money.

2. _____
   A. John asked, "When will we go to the library to get a new book?"
   B. "Have you already finished the last ones", asked his mom.
   C. "Yes, and I have another book report due in two weeks."
   D. Mom replied, "Get your things. We'll go now."

3. _____
   A. The three largest planets are Jupiter, Saturn, and Neptune.
   B. Our solar system contains, our sun, nine planets, many moons, comets, and meteorites.
   C. Mercury is the closest planet to the sun, but Venus is hotter because of its greenhouse effect.
   D. Earth is the only planet in our solar system with conditions suitable for humans to live.

4. _____
   A. She is an intelligent, creative, responsible student.
   B. Her favorite classes are English, science, and history.
   C. On our way into school this morning we stopped for doughnuts.
   D. The weather was crisp, cool, and sunny.

5. _____
   A. Jose Rojas who is in my history class is going to Florida State University next year.
   B. I applied to Princeton, Harvard, and Stanford, but I don't know if I'll be accepted.
   C. Colleges consider grades, standardized test scores, writing samples, and recommendations before accepting potential students.
   D. One of my strengths is my participation in activities, including soccer, the newspaper, the yearbook, student government, volunteer in a city elementary school, and environmental club.

6. _____
   A. At the age of 39, Franklin Delano Roosevelt was stricken with polio.
   B. Roosevelt became the only person in history to be elected to four terms as President of the United States.
   C. Coming from a prominent New York family, Roosevelt graduated from Harvard College and Columbia Law School.
   D. The strains of World War II aggravated Roosevelt's high blood pressure, and heart condition and resulted in his death in 1945.

3-8A. Continued

7. _____

    A. On an August weekend in 1969, about 400,000 people came to a rock concert called Woodstock.

    B. The musicians included Janis Joplin, Joan Baez, Jimi Hendrix, and the Jefferson Airplane.

    C. Lack of preparation for the large crowds resulted in shortages of food and water, shelter from the rain, and bathrooms.

    D. Despite the mud, rain, and other problems most people were happy to just listen to the music.

8. _____

    A. On July 20, 1969 millions of people watched on TV as the Apollo 11 space mission landed a human on the moon.

    B. Neil Armstrong, Edwin E. Aldrin, and Michael Collins were members of the Apollo 11 crew.

    C. As he climbed down the ladder, Neil Armstrong announced, "That's one small step for man, one giant leap for mankind."

    D. President Nixon told the astronauts, "For every American, this has to be the proudest day of our lives."

9. _____

    A. In 1989, the *Exxon Valdez* struck a reef and spilled 11 million gallons of oil into Prince William Sound, Alaska.

    B. Thousands of animals were killed, including ducks, eagles, otters, seals, salmon, and herring.

    C. Volunteers worked to clean the gooey oil from animals, rocks, and water.

    D. Cold temperatures, and wet conditions made the cleanup very difficult.

10. _____

    A. The ocean floor contains mountains, canyons, and plains even larger than those on land.

    B. The deepest place in the oceans, is about 7 miles down in the Mariana Trench in the Pacific Ocean.

    C. Also found in the Pacific is the Ring of Fire, an area of great volcanic activity.

    D. The Mid-Atlantic Ridge, a huge chain of mountains, is found on the bottom of the Atlantic Ocean.

11. _____

    A. The capital of the United States is Washington, D.C., located on the east coast.

    B. Mt. McKinley, the highest point in the U.S. at 6,194 miles, is in Alaska.

    C. Mt. Waialeale, the wettest place in the U.S., has an annual rainfall of 460 inches.

    D. Most of Alaska averages a population density of under 3 people per square mile

3-8A. Continued

12. _____

    A. In studying grammar it is essential that you know, the parts of speech.

    B. Nouns, verbs, and adjectives are the first to learn.

    C. Identification of adverbs, prepositions, conjunctions, and interjections come later in your study.

    D. Pronouns and articles were the easiest for me to learn.

13. _____

    A. Mercury, Venus, Earth, and Mars are the terrestrial planets, meaning that they are made of rock.

    B. Jupiter, Saturn, Uranus, Neptune, and Pluto are Jovian planets, all, except Pluto, having a composition consisting mainly of hydrogen.

    C. Jupiter is a giant planet, larger than all the other planets put together.

    D. The Giant Red Spot on Jupiter, is a huge storm that measures more that 15,000 miles across.

14. _____

    A. Water is the only substance on earth that exists naturally as a solid, a liquid, and a gas.

    B. Water is a compound made up of hydrogen and oxygen.

    C. A natural solvent water is used to clean many things.

    D. Some of the physical properties of water include colorless, odorless, tasteless, has surface tension, and cohesion.

15. _____

    A. The Earth's crust is divided into 15 plates which float on the mantle, causing earthquakes and volcanic eruptions when they move.

    B. The edges of the plates are areas of the greatest seismic and volcanic activity.

    C. About 200 million years ago, all the continents were joined together to form a supercontinent called Pangea.

    D. Today North America is moving away from Europe at a rate of about 1 inch per year

3-8B. IDENTIFYING PUNCTUATION ERRORS

Activity: Choose the sentence in each set that contains a punctuation error.

1. _____
   A. I love ice cream very much and I like peanut butter too.
   B. Off she went in a new car.
   C. Everyone seemed excited about their weekend adventures.
   D. The event had finally arrived.

2. _____
   A. "Stop talking!" shouted the impatient teacher.
   B. This is the best option, and I think you ought to accept the offer.
   C. "Go now!" he ordered.
   D. Jake replied, "I believe youre correct."

3. _____
   A. She arrived sooner than expected.
   B. Mary Ellen responded quickly to the request.
   C. Are you aware of your choices.
   D. I think you ought to try that option.

4. _____
   A. She left at 8 A.M., and she arrived at noon.
   B. The woman left for the beach, and arrived later than expected.
   C. Go now!
   D. We waited for three hours, and then the bus arrived.

5. _____
   A. "I like your answer," she retorted.
   B. "That's a great idea," exclaimed the manager!
   C. "I have a new barbecue, and I'd like to demonstrate how it works," Tim chimed in.
   D. "Who's going?" Dad asked.

6. _____
   A. We cant believe your answer.
   B. Is that really the situation?
   C. Who knows better than I do?
   D. Haven't you seen the newspaper today?

3-8B. Continued

7. _____

    A. Mary, you did a fine job.

    B. I am not sure of your answer Mark.

    C. Go, Claude, before we change our minds.

    D. Did Harry find the answer yet?

8. _____

    A. Is that yours or mine?

    B. Go now before it's too late!

    C. Bring this paper to your friend over there.

    D. Youre wrong!

9. _____

    A. John, a good friend of mine, is captain of the soccer team.

    B. Give this to Mary, the secretary on the third floor.

    C. Harvard, a famous university has a fine reputation.

    D. Did you see Andrew or Sara today?

10. _____

    A. Fifty percent of those surveyed responded.

    B. For dinner you will need these items; potatoes, milk, rolls and butter.

    C. Bring this over to your brother's home.

    D. Ginger, I've found your long-lost locket.

3-9. A STRATEGY FOR IDENTIFYING CORRECT PUNCTUATION

On a standardized or classroom test, you are sometimes called upon to identify the correct use of punctuation. In this activity you will focus specifically on the use of apostrophes and quotation marks.

Example: 1. Which of the following sentences is correctly punctuated?
  A. Anton's favorite book is *The Adventures of Tom Sawyer.*
  B. Samuel Clemens' had Tom and Huck in many adventures.
  C. Toms' sense of adventure keeps the reader interested.
  D. Many reader's choose this novel as one of their favorites.

Explanation: The correct choice here is A since an apostrophe is used to show ownership. Since the book belongs to Anton, an apostrophe and an *s* are needed.

TESTING TIP:

Remember to use apostrophes in contractions and to show ownership. Use quotation marks to indicate a person's exact words as well as titles. Review the rules if necessary.

3-9A. IDENTIFYING CORRECT PUNCTUATION

Activity: Choose the sentence in each set that is correctly punctuated.

1. _____
- A. The eagle built it's nest in the highest possible place to protect its young.
- B. The osprey's fish was stolen in flight by a bald eagle.
- C. The golden eagles prey includes rabbits, woodchucks, and other small mammals.
- D. The bald eagles wingspan is more than 7 feet.

2. _____
- A. John asked, "Whats for dinner?"
- B. Sara replied "Chicken, mashed potatoes, and peas."
- C. "I had chicken for lunch today," mumbled John.
- D. "Then you can have it twice or make something yourself", suggested Sara.

3. _____
- A. We're going to have Thanksgiving dinner at my grandparents house.
- B. Havent you turned off the TV yet?
- C. We couldn't get to the store because the car's battery died.
- D. Im on my way to the library to check out some new books.

4. _____
- A. Harry said, "Last Halloween I was a pumpkin, but this year I'm going to be a ghost."
- B. Lucy added, "I'm going to be a mummy wrapped in strips of cloth and I'm going to carry a mummys chain to rattle."
- C. "Mummies don't rattle chains. Ghosts are the ones with chains", said Rosa.
- D. "Well, maybe so, but my mummys going to have a chain, too." Lucy stubbornly insisted.

5. _____
- A. Phillip's photographs of the class trip made everyone laugh.
- B. One picture showed Billys jacket left on a fence.
- C. Another showed the cow's in the Millers' field with Joe making faces at them.
- D. A huge pile of the students backpacks was artistically next to a pile of pumpkins.

6. _____
- A. The teacher said, "finish this assignment."
- B. The student replied that "He didn't understand the directions."
- C. "Let me explain," she began, "so that you can do it on your own."
- D. "Now it makes sense. Thanks", said Harry.

7. _____
- A. Mary said "Let's go to the mall."
- B. "Okay," replied Sam, "I need to get a new sweater."
- C. "Stuart's is having a big sale today" interrupted Sally.
- D. "Then what are we waiting for," asked Mary?

3-9A. Continued

8. _____
    A. "I hope," said Gary, "that I can fall asleep quickly tonight".
    B. Donna asked, "Have you been having problems sleeping"?
    C. "My cold and stuffy nose keep me from breathing at night", replied Gary.
    D. "Try a hot shower and then a cup of warm milk," suggested Donna.

9. _____
    A. The girls soccer team won the county tournament.
    B. My sisters' job is a secretary to a judge.
    C. The jury did it's best to be fair.
    D. The baby's toys all fit inside the toy chest before we began playing.

10. _____
    A. The lawyer's office is on Broad Street.
    B. This assignment will take you five minute's work.
    C. Niraj and my report's was on volcanoes.
    D. I thought the top score on the math test was her's.

11. _____
    A. Mrs. Chang announced, "that there will be a test on Tuesday."
    B. Ashley responded, "We have a science quiz and a math test scheduled for that day".
    C. Then Mrs. Chang said, "In that case, I'll make our history test on Wednesday."
    D. The students all said "Thank you."

12. _____
    A. "I can hardly wait until summer vacation" muttered Patrick.
    B. Cynthia laughed, "but it's only November."
    C. "I like to plan ahead. It gives me a goal answered Patrick."
    D. "How about making straight A's until Thanksgiving as your goal?" suggested Cynthia.

13. _____
    A. My math teachers name is Mrs. Jones.
    B. The ski school trained it's instructors during summer.
    C. Mary was very flattered to be named in the book's dedication.
    D. Fluffys' collar was too loose and it slipped off.

14. _____
    A. The weather forecaster's report called for 6 inches of snow.
    B. *The Farmer's Almanac* predicted the winters total accumulation to be 6 inches.
    C. The newspapers' report said we would have 8 to 12 inches.
    D. Joes' Uncle Harry was right with his amateur prediction of 2 inches.

15. _____
    A. Amy mumbled, "I wish I could get better grades in math"
    B. "Sarah offered to help with homework assignments."
    C. Amy asked Mr. Grant "if he could help her after school, too."
    D. Finally, Amy said happily, "After all that work, I raised my grade to a B+."

3-10. A STRATEGY FOR IDENTIFYING USAGE ERRORS

On a standardized or classroom test, you are sometimes called upon to identify errors in usage.

Example: 1.   Which of the following sentences contains a usage error?
  A. The new movie might of been a hit if the lead actor were better.
  B. He could've performed better in the stunts of this action thriller.
  C. His co-star is a talented well-known actress who should have given him better support.
  D. She could've made the difference.

Explanation: The correct choice here is A since the expression *might of* is improper and should be the contracton for *might have* or *might've*.

TESTING TIP:

Since usage errors are often commonly used in spoken language, they may be difficult for you to identify. Remember, tests are based on formal written language. Review the rules if necessary.

Name_____ Date_____

3-10A. IDENTIFYING USAGE ERRORS

Activity: Choose the sentence in each set that contains an error in usage.

1. _____
   A. If it hadn't rained, we might of won the game.
   B. I could have gone if you had asked me.
   C. We would have sent a present, but we had no money.
   D. She should have apologized.

2. _____
   A. Joe is the oldest boy in his class.
   B. Between my brother and me, I am the biggest.
   C. In the Great Turtle Race, Speedy was slower than Snoopy.
   D. The longest book I ever read was *Tom Sawyer*.

3. _____
   A. An argument began among the two brothers.
   B. My choice was between a vacation in the Bahamas and going to summer school.
   C. The prize was to be split among six winners.
   D. I searched everywhere for the cat.

4. _____
   A. Mary excepted my apology.
   B. No one except Jeff knew the secret code.
   C. The police officer said he was not allowed to accept gifts.
   D. I learned all of the poem except the last verse.

5. _____
   A. In the soccer tournament, we played a good game and won.
   B. The team played well again on Saturday.
   C. I went to the doctor because I did not feel well.
   D. After her art classes, Sarah could paint good.

6. _____
   A. He jumped off of the diving board and into the pool.
   B. There is a slide outside the building.
   C. Take the book off the shelf if you want to see it.
   D. Rachel slid off the horse onto the ground.

7. _____
   A. I read that the Giants might make the playoffs.
   B. I really like them football players.
   C. A lunar eclipse is when the earth's shadow falls on the moon.
   D. I saw those famous people on the news report.

159

3-10A. Continued

8. _____

    A. The message was for my brother and I.

    B. Melissa and I froze during the football game.

    C. Between you and me, I think Sam is the smartest kid in class.

    D. Gary, Seth, and I competed in the school track meet.

9. _____

    A. Let me go with you this time.

    B. Leave them find their own ride home.

    C. Will Jim let you borrow his jacket?

    D. Don't leave before two o'clock.

10. _____

    A. I could not find my homework anywheres.

    B. Everywhere I looked, I came up empty.

    C. It was just nowhere to be found.

    D. Finally, I found it just where it belonged—in my notebook.

3-11. A STRATEGY FOR IDENTIFYING CORRECT USAGE

On a standardized or classroom test, you are sometimes called upon to identify correct usage.

Example: 1. Which of the following sentences has correct usage?
  A. The prisoner had to accept his fate and face three years in jail.
  B. All of the assigned books had been read during the summer accept one.
  C. Public officials should not except gifts or bribes.
  D. His name was accepted from the birthday party list after his temper tantrum.

Explanation: The correct choice here is A since the word *accept* is properly used. *Accept* means to take or acknowledge, whereas *except* means to leave out.

TESTING TIP:

Since usage errors are often commonly used in spoken language, they may be difficult for you to identify. Remember, tests are based on formal written language. Review the rules if necessary.

3-11A. IDENTIFYING CORRECT USAGE

Activity: Choose the sentence in each set that demonstrates correct usage.

1. _____
   A. The secret was between Joe and I.
   B. The decision was between Mary, Sara, and Jose.
   C. Among the group, Harry was the only one to make the honor roll.
   D. John and I could only come up with $3 among us.

2. _____
   A. Me and my friends are going to the movie.
   B. Mary and me go to the mall every Saturday.
   C. My sister and I then meet my parents and we all have pizza together.
   D. My mother wants to drive Mary and I home together.

3. _____
   A. The kids on the basketball team talked between themselves.
   B. There was an agreement among the two tallest players.
   C. They would pass the ball between them until Joey got under the basket.
   D. Then they would pass the ball among the whole team until Joey got a shot.

4. _____
   A. Jeffrey doesn't study enough to do well on tests.
   B. He don't put in enough time at home.
   C. He and Sara doesn't turn off the music while they work.
   D. He don't eliminate distractions.

5. _____
   A. I went to the nurse because I didn't feel good.
   B. I tried out my new bicycle and it went good.
   C. He was a good person to give back the money he found.
   D. Even though we played good, we lost the game.

6. _____
   A. Younger then Manuel, Jose was the youngest in his family.
   B. Than the baby was born to make Jose the middle child.
   C. Though younger, Jose was taller then Manuel.
   D. But Manuel was heavier than Jose by 20 pounds.

7. _____
   A. The dog who barked at me is usually very friendly.
   B. There is the man which owns him.
   C. He also has a parrot who is very talkative.
   D. The parrot has a cage which is four feet high.

3-11A. Continued

8. _____
    A. The movie has lots of terrific special effects.
    B. The director wanted to have an affect on his audience.
    C. The blood and gore seemed to affect a lot of people.
    D. Unfortunately, his affect was too great and no one liked the movie.

9. _____
    A. We could have gone skiing this weekend.
    B. We should of checked the weather first.
    C. Then we might of known it would be okay to drive by Saturday.
    D. But then, we would of missed the horror movie on TV.

10. _____
    A. Will your parents leave you go to the dance?
    B. My mother never lets me do anything I want.
    C. Leave the tangled bird free when you loosen the string.
    D. Let me alone so I can read.

SECTION FOUR

Writing

COMPOSITION
WRITING SAMPLES AND OPEN-ENDED RESPONSES

COMPOSITION

Standardized and classroom tests often use similar vocabulary when presenting test questions and directions. Familiarity with these words and phrasings can be helpful when taking such tests. Increased understanding of these words and phrases will help you in responding to such test questions.

Here are some common directions used on tests specific to written composition:

- Choose the sentence that best states the idea.
- Choose the sentence that best combines the underlined sentences into one.
- Choose the opening sentence that is supported by the details in the paragraph.
- Choose the details that best support the main idea.
- Which of the following topics does not belong in the following passage?
- Which of the following would be most appropriate to include in the following passage?
- This is a list of the major topics in the passage. Which of the following shows the parts of this outline arranged in the correct order?
- Which of the following sentences expresses the idea most clearly and logically?
- Which of the following best expresses the author's purpose?
- If the statements above are true, which of the following is necessarily true?
- Which of the following details would be least effective in the passage?
- Choose the word that would best complete the sentence.
- The terms in each set of brackets are related mainly because ___.
- Which of the following words can be used to describe the others?
- Which of the following is the best heading for the others?
- Which of the following would be least likely to follow the opening sentence above?
- Which of the following would most likely come after the last sentence in the passage?
- Find the best order for arranging the sentences into a paragraph.
- Which of the following words should the author use in the sentence below to make the reader feel that the character is angry?
- Which of the following would be the best sentence to help make the character's feelings come to life?
- Which of the following sentences would best link the two paragraphs in the passage?
- Which of the following sentences would best end the passage?
- The information in this passage would be most suitable for the students in a ___ class.
- The voice of the writer of this passage is most like that of a ___.
- Which of the following would be the best first sentence for the passage?
- Which of the following sentences could be added after sentence number ___?
- Which of the following sentences could begin the ___ paragraph?
- Which group of words would be more colorful than the words ___ in sentence number ___?
- Which sentence does not belong in the story?
- Which group of words repeats an idea when it is not necessary?
- Why is ___ writing this letter?
- Which sentence does not belong in the letter?

© 1997 by John Wiley & Sons Inc

4-1. A STRATEGY FOR SELECTING THE TOPIC SENTENCE

In a well-written paragraph the first sentence usually introduces the topic or states the main idea. The sentences that follow generally include details or examples to support or explain that topic or main idea. On a standardized or classroom test you may be given a paragraph with no topic sentence and then be asked to choose the best topic sentence from a list of several.

Example: _____. There was a flurry of activity on the beach as the vacationers quickly gathered their belongings and took down their umbrellas. The wind had been kicking up for a while, and the storm clouds were moving swiftly overhead. The boaters could be seen quickly heading toward the bay and struggling to maintain course.

    A.   People could be seen gathering up their children and heading toward their cars.

    B.   Lifeguards were signaling for all bathers to come ashore.

    C.   A bolt of lightning streaked across the sky followed by a crack of thunder.

    D.   A beautiful beach day had been interrupted by the threat of an oncoming storm.

Explanation: The first three choices above are detail sentences because they list additional events. The fourth sentence, however, introduces the topic of the paragraph. Since all of the remaining sentences tell of the specific results of the storm, the opening sentence must introduce the main idea. In this case, the main idea is the storm's arrival and effect on the vacationers.

TESTING TIP:

Read the details of the paragraph. Ask yourself what is the point of this paragraph as you try to determine the main idea. Then read the sentence choices to find the best introductory sentence.

4-1A. SELECTING THE TOPIC SENTENCE

Activity: Choose the opening sentence that goes best with the details in the paragraph.

1. _____. Water is one factor that is necessary for growth. A plant will wilt and be unable to carry on photosynthesis without sufficient water. Another factor that affects growth is temperature. Within an ideal temperature range, plants will grow, increasing the rate of growth with an increase in temperature. But if temperatures are too high or too low, growth will stop and the plant may even die. Light is necessary for plant growth. Without enough light, plants cannot carry on photosynthesis. Neighboring plants may shade or crowd a growing plant, resulting in limited growth.

   A. There are several factors that may affect the growth of a plant.
   B. If temperatures are too low, a plant may freeze and die.
   C. The length of daylight determines when a plant will produce a flower.
   D. Too much water may rot the roots and cause a plant to die.

2. _____. When school let out, he was scheduled to join a wilderness adventure group to camp and experience the outdoors in Wyoming. Hiking, bicycling, mountain climbing, swimming, and camping were among his favorite activities. The trip would also include a survival and a climbing challenge. Jamie was sure this would be a trip of a lifetime.

   A. Jamie had been camping with his family since he was a toddler.
   B. Jamie loved to camp.
   C. Jamie had never been to Wyoming before.
   D. Jamie expected this summer vacation to be his best ever.

3. _____. *Sputnik* became a symbol of America's place of superiority in the world. This event served to give America a purpose. That purpose was to beat the Russians in science and technology. The conquest of space became a national goal as the two countries battled for superiority. Finally in 1969, America landed Apollo 11 on the surface of the moon and took the lead in the race for space.

   A. Nikita Khrushchev was the leader of Russia in 1957.
   B. In 1957 the Russians launched *Sputnik,* the first satellite which launched the United States into the space race.
   C. The 1950s was a time of prosperity for the United States.
   D. The Apollo spacecraft program played an important role in American space technology.

4. _____. The party would be held at Jason's house because he had a large swimming pool. Sara, Lauren, and Sam volunteered to take care of the food. Jamie, Pat, and Alex said they would supply the equipment for volleyball and pool basketball. Mo wanted to take care of the music. Soon, everyone had volunteered to help in some way. Within ten minutes everything was arranged for what promised to be a great way to end the school year.

   A. All the students wanted to help.
   B. Everyone hoped it would be a hot, sunny day.
   C. The class eagerly planned their year-end party.
   D. The class then had the enthusiasm needed to finish the last two weeks of classes.

4-1A. Continued

5. _____. This octopus lives in the western Pacific from Australia to southern Japan. Surprisingly, the blue-ringed octopus is small, having arms about three inches long. Like most octopuses, it is shy and prefers to hide or crawl away from humans. To protect itself if stepped on or picked up, the blue-ringed octopus bites and injects saliva so poisonous that it can kill an adult in a very short time. Fortunately, quick medical treatment can prevent death.

   A. Although small, the blue-ringed octopus has a powerful defense mechanism.

   B. All octopuses have eight arms with about 240 suction cups.

   C. All octopuses taste with their suction cups.

   D. The arms of the Pacific octopus can reach 30 feet.

Extension: Not all paragraphs begin with an introductory sentence that states the main idea of the paragraph. Use a science or social studies textbook to find at least three paragraphs that begin with a main idea sentence. You may need to read several paragraphs before you find three organized in this way.

4-2. A STRATEGY FOR WRITING TOPIC SENTENCES

In a well-written paragraph the first sentence usually introduces the topic or states the main idea. The sentences that follow generally include details or examples to support or explain that topic or main idea. You can strengthen your ability to identify topic sentences as well as develop stronger writing skills by practicing how to write effective topic sentences.

Example: Read the following detail and/or example sentences. Determine the general topic or main idea. Then write a sentence containing that main idea which will introduce the paragraph.

_____. Once you arrive, you must first get on the rental line in order to be <u>properly fitted</u> for ski boots, skis, and poles. This usually takes some time. Once you have been fitted, you move on to <u>the lift ticket line</u> where you purchase either a half- or full-day lift ticket. Then you take all your equipment outside with you and <u>ready yourself for a day of fun</u>.

Explanation: The paragraph above talks mainly about the preparation necessary for a ski trip. Since the details discuss the equipment and procedures for getting started, you will need a topic sentence that introduces that idea.

Topic Sentence: _____

_____

TESTING TIP:

Underline the key words and phrases in each of the detail sentences of the paragraph. Then think about how these words and phrases are related. Write a topic sentence that helps prepare the reader to understand this relationship.

4-2A. WRITING TOPIC SENTENCES

Activity: Write an opening sentence for each of the following paragraphs. Remember to use key words and phrases to help you write your sentence.

1. _____. The day had been filled with dramatic weather conditions for the region. A tornado had been reported in the suburban communities beyond the river. Thunder and lightning could be seen and heard, and a teeming rainstorm caused the banks of the river to flood. The weather forecasters on the local news shows said that the weather conditions would be likely to continue for several more hours.

_____

_____

2. _____. Timothy and Christopher played on the fall soccer league and had spent many hours perfecting their kicking game. In the winter season, both boys turned to the town's recreation basketball league. Many practice hours help them to improve their shooting and endurance. In spring, Timothy headed for the tennis courts while Christopher went in for swimming.

_____

_____

3. _____. You could see that Nicole had been practicing her ballet for many months. As you watched her in the day's recital, her gracefulness was most evident. She moved about on stage with ease. Her jumps seemed effortless, and her fine position further emphasized her developing artistry.

_____

_____

4. _____. By the age of two, Lindsay was often seen playing with her brothers. For example, when Timothy and Chris were out on the driveway playing street hockey, Lindsay could be seen running to catch the hockey puck. When the boys took off for the swing set, she would be seen running right behind. If her brothers were playing one of the video games, you could be sure that Lindsay would be looking for a third hand control.

_____

_____

5. _____. The custodians could be seen polishing the floors of the school and putting the finishing touches on the windows. The main office was filled with activity. Teachers were organizing their students' materials and preparing the many bulletin boards. The trees in front of the school were beginning to change color as a crispness could be felt in the air.

_____

_____

Extension: Think of an activity that you enjoy doing and the steps necessary to complete it. Then write a paragraph containing an effective topic sentence and several supporting detail sentences.

4-3. A STRATEGY FOR SELECTING SUPPORTING DETAILS

In a well-written paragraph the first sentence usually introduces the topic or states the main idea. The sentences that follow generally include details or examples to support or explain that topic or main idea.

Example: Read the following main idea sentence. Then read the choices that follow and decide which sentence best supports that main idea.

Main Idea: Camouflage is an excellent defense.
A. The cheetah can run faster than its prey for short distances. It can reach sixty-five miles per hour but will give up if it can't catch its prey within a short distance.
B. The great white shark has razor sharp teeth capable of crushing bone and tearing the strongest of muscles in its prey. One of its favorite prey is the sea lion.
C. Beige and brown markings of the common toad enable it to hide undetected as its predator scans the ground for food. Combined with its ability to remain motionless, the toad will often escape detection.
D. Poison arrow frogs have bright warning colors to alert predators of their danger. Poison from their backs is rubbed on darts to make them deadly hunting tools.

Explanation: The main idea of this paragraph is the use of camouflage as a defense. While the first and second choices discuss animal defenses, they do not focus on camouflage. The fourth choice discusses coloration but again does not discuss camouflage. The third choice is the correct one as it explains how the toad uses camouflage to escape its predator.

TESTING TIP:

Underline the key words and/or phrases in each of the choices. Determine the relationship among them and use this relationship to choose the best support for the main idea sentence.

4-3A. SELECTING SUPPORTING DETAILS

Activity: Read the following main idea sentences. Then read the choices that follow and decide which sentence best supports that particular main idea.

1. *Main Idea:*   Sports today present safety risks to those involved.
    A. During the fall of each year, the sport of football surrounds us. Hours of televised high school, college, and professional football games enter our family rooms each weekend.
    B. Horse racing is a very popular sport today. Both the horse owners and the jockeys have been known to earn in the six figures annually.
    C. Skateboarding has become extremely popular in the 1990s. With its increased popularity has come some hazards as well. Elbow, knee, and head injuries have sent many skateboarders to the hospital for treatment.
    D. Ice skating increases in popularity following each winter Olympics. Following the Olympics, many youngsters can be seen flocking to their local sporting goods stores to purchase a new pair of ice skates.

2. *Main Idea:*   Today's technology has provided a variety of alternatives for long distance communication.
    A. The American Pony Express was one of our earliest vehicles for long distance communication. For that period of our history, it was an important way for people to communicate with each other.
    B. Fax machines and electronic mail permit instant communication at a relatively low cost to almost anywhere. Many more Americans are taking advantage of these forms of communication.
    C. Long distance phone bills can be expensive. For those who have relatives living on the other side of the country or somewhere in the international community, frequent phone calls can add up.
    D. Cable television has brought many more viewing stations into our homes today. It is not unusual for today's television viewer to choose from more than fifty programs when tuning in.

3. *Main Idea:*   Summer is a time when Americans relax and enjoy themselves.
    A. Summer weather in the East is often characterized by hot and humid conditions. Many find this weather pattern uncomfortable and retreat to the indoors.
    B. It is not uncommon for families to schedule their vacations during the summer. For some families vacations take them far away while others remain closer to home. Whatever the case, Americans have a more relaxed lifestyle at this time of year and find many ways to involve themselves in recreational activities.
    C. On a summer evening, the nation's highways often resemble parking lots. This can sometimes try the patience of even the calmest of people. Avoid traveling the nation's highways if you can.
    D. An increasing number of school districts around our country have converted to year-round school scheduling. This has had its advantages and disadvantages. Children in one family may not be on the same schedule. This often creates a problem for families who want to take a summer vacation together.

4-3A. Continued

4. *Main Idea:*   Over the years travel has become more convenient.
   A. Today's airlines feature more efficient airplanes. Not only are they increasingly safer, but they also travel at higher speeds. This, of course, shortens the time it takes to get from one location to another and is important to many travelers.
   B. A drive by the auto dealers on any of America's highways will reveal the great variety of automobiles available today. The shapes, colors, and features are endless and often confuse the auto shopper.
   C. Many vacationers choose to travel by ship today. They especially enjoy the entertainment and food buffets found on such cruises.
   D. Traveling our country by bus today has both its advantages and disadvantages. One of the many disadvantages is the frequent stops the bus usually must make as it travels between one point and its final destination. The frequent stopping and going is disturbing to those who try to sleep while traveling.

5. *Main Idea:*   Children's birthday parties today are quite different from those of the past.
   A. Birthdays are important occasions and worth the effort involved in planning a celebration party. I especially like to have the candles that can't be blown out.
   B. One of the first difficulties is preparing the list of invited guests. It is often hard to know who to invite. Then once you've organized your list, it takes a while before everyone responds and you know who is coming.
   C. Many people choose to have their birthday parties at a place other than their homes. Skating rinks, children's gyms, and restaurants are some examples.
   D. I remember my favorite birthday party. All of my relatives attended. It was in our backyard, and we played my favorite game—"pin the tale on the donkey."

4-4. ANOTHER STRATEGY FOR SELECTING SUPPORTING DETAILS

In a well-written paragraph the first sentence usually introduces the topic or states the main idea. The sentences that follow generally include details or examples to support or explain that topic or main idea. In some standardized or classroom tests you may be asked to identify detail sentences that do not belong in the paragraph. Sometimes the main idea sentence is included and sometimes it is not.

Example: Read the following paragraph. Determine the general topic or main idea. Then read the supporting sentences, checking each one to be sure that it supports the main idea.

(1) Niko was quite nervous on his first day at his new school. (2) For the first four years of his school career, Niko attended Western Elementary School and had developed many fine friendships. (3) He could hardly eat breakfast that morning and nearly missed the bus. (4) His mother had packed him a ham and cheese sandwich. (5) He sat quietly on the bus while the other children talked about their summer vacations. (6) Once at school, Niko found his way to his classroom and again felt very alone.

Explanation: The paragraph above talks mainly about Niko's nervousness on his first day at his new school. All of the sentences following this main idea sentence support the topic. However, sentence 4 provides unrelated information; what he had for lunch does not add to why he was nervous.

TESTING TIP:

Underline the key words and phrases in each of the detail sentences of the paragraph. Then think about whether these words and phrases are related to the main idea. This will help you determine the unrelated information.

Name_____ Date_____

4-4A. SELECTING SUPPORTING DETAILS

Activity: Read the following paragraph. The general topic or main idea appears in the first sentence. Then read the supporting sentences, checking each one to be sure that it supports the main idea. Identify the sentence that does not support the main idea.

1. Rafflesia, which grows in the jungle, is one of the world's most unusual plants. (1) The flower of the rafflesia is three feet across. (2) In bloom, the rafflesia smells like rotten hamburger. (3) This rotten smell attracts flies to the rafflesia which pick up its pollen. (4) Like many other plants, the rafflesia depends on insects.
   A. Sentence 1   C. Sentence 3
   B. Sentence 2   D. Sentence 4

2. Bats play a very helpful role in an ecosystem, but many people are frightened by them. (1) Horror stories about vampire bats have made many people scared of being attacked. (2) In reality, most bats serve a very helpful purpose by eating thousands of insects each night. (3) Bats find their prey through echo location. (4) Some kinds of bats pollinate flowers and others spread seeds after eating fruit.
   A. Sentence 1   C. Sentence 3
   B. Sentence 2   D. Sentence 4

3. The plants in a tropical rain forest form layers as they compete with each other for sunlight. (1) The taller trees get the most sunlight and spread out to let their leaves get as much sun as possible. (2) One kind of bamboo can grow nearly two feet a day until it reaches about 100 feet. (3) The branches of tall trees make a thick layer called the canopy. (4) The lower trees form the understory, a layer of shorter, shrubby growth.
   A. Sentence 1   C. Sentence 3
   B. Sentence 2   D. Sentence 4

4. Tropical rain forests provide many products we take for granted. (1) There are more different kinds of plants and animals living in the rain forest than in the rest of the world. (2) Chocolate, cinnamon, vanilla, and kola used to flavor cola soft drinks were all discovered growing in the rain forest. (3) Jungle plants provide medicines and wood. (4) Rubber also comes from trees that grow in the tropical forests.
   A. Sentence 1   C. Sentence 3
   B. Sentence 2   D. Sentence 4

5. Although termites are pests in our homes, they are helpful in the rain forest. (1) As termites eat, they help recycle dead wood. (2) Their nests may be taller than four feet. (3) By chewing up old wood, the termites help turn wood into food for fungus, bacteria, and small animals. (4) Without termites and other insects, dead trees and other plants would pile up to smother the rain forest.
   A. Sentence 1   C. Sentence 3
   B. Sentence 2   D. Sentence 4

Name_____ Date_____

4-4A. Continued

6. Forests are filled with an incredible array of wildlife. (1) On the forest floor a close look will reveal an army of insects that thrives on the dead leaves and branches that have fallen. (2) Mushrooms, fungi, and moss can also be seen in this part of the forest community. (3) Of course, there are many varieties of animals that inhabit the forest as well. (4) You might spot a small animal like a raccoon as well as a larger animal like a deer. (5) Our forests are sometimes threatened by fires during the dry months of the year.

   A. Sentence 2   C. Sentence 5

   B. Sentence 4   D. Sentence 6

7. Breakfast is an important meal of the day. (1) Orange, pineapple, or some other juice is frequently seen on the breakfast menu. (2) Both hot and cold cereals are often a main part of a breakfast meal. (3) Eggs, sausage, and bacon are commonly seen on the breakfast table and are served in many ways. (4) The price of a breakfast varies from place to place. (5) Breakfast is the meal that gets you off to a strong start for the day.

   A. Sentence 1   C. Sentence 4

   B. Sentence 3   D. Sentence 5

8. Americans live in a wide variety of housing styles. (1) For those living in one of our cities, the apartment is a common home for many. (2) Choosing a home is not easy. (3) Town homes have also become quite popular. (4) These are usually two- or three-story homes that are attached to each other. (5) The single-family home continues to be a popular choice for many. (6) Single-family homes come in ranch, split level, colonial, and contemporary designs and are usually surrounded by a private yard.

   A. Sentence 1   C. Sentence 4

   B. Sentence 2   D. Sentence 5

9. A visit to the movie theater today offers the viewer a wide variety of choices. (1) Action-packed thrillers continue to attract a good share of the movie-going public. (2) Of course, there are always those films that tell a compelling personal story. (3) The cost of movies has skyrocketed in recent years. (4) For the younger audience, there is a variety of entertaining movies available. (5) For those who enjoy a good laugh, comedies are a popular choice. (6) Regardless of the viewer's preference on any day, there is likely to be a movie out there to fill the bill!

   A. Sentence 1   C. Sentence 3

   B. Sentence 2   D. Sentence 5

Extension: Select one of the questions above. On the back of this sheet, explain your reasoning for choosing the answer you did.

4-5. A STRATEGY FOR SEQUENCING IDEAS

In a well-written paragraph the first sentence usually introduces the topic or states the main idea. The sentences that follow generally include details or examples to support or explain that topic or main idea. These details or examples are arranged in a logical order so that the reader can follow the author's ideas. The arrangement of details can follow various patterns. The most common is the chronological or time order. That will be our focus here.

Example: Read the following sentences.
1. All of the guests greatly enjoyed the delicious food.
2. Diana carried the tray of hamburgers and hot dogs to the table.
3. Colorful place settings awaited the guests.
4. John cleared the table and did the dishes.

Determine which order of the following sentences is most logical.
A. 3, 1, 2, 4
B. 3, 2, 1, 4
C. 4, 3, 2, 1
D. 3, 4, 2, 1

Explanation: The correct arrangement in this case is B. This is the most logical order of events for these choices. If you read the events in any other order, you will see that one event cannot take place until another has already happened.

TESTING TIP:

When given a question of this type, it is often helpful to determine the first sentence in the sequence of events. Once you have done this, you can then eliminate those choices in which that sentence is not first. In the example above, choice C can be eliminated early since clearing the table would obviously come last. In the same way, if you know the last step in the sequence, you may be able to eliminate choices.

4-5A. SEQUENCING IDEAS

Activity: Read the following sentences. Determine the general topic or main idea. Then read the supporting sentences, checking each one to be sure that it supports the main idea.

1. Read the following sentences.
    1. He named his puppy Spike.
    2. Last summer Ricardo got a new puppy for his birthday.
    3. It took Ricardo a long time to house train Spike.
    4. Spike was the star graduate at obedience school.

    Determine which order of the following sentences is most logical.
    A. 1, 3, 2, 4
    B. 2, 1, 3, 4
    C. 4, 2, 3, 1
    D. 2, 4, 1, 3

2. Read the following sentences.
    1. The invention of the VCR enabled us to watch movies on our television sets.
    2. The invention of the radio enabled people to hear news and entertainment in their homes instantly.
    3. The invention of the television enabled people to see as well as hear entertainment in their homes.
    4. The installation of electricity into homes began a series of inventions that Benjamin Franklin could never have imagined.

    Determine which order of the following sentences is most logical.
    A. 4, 1, 2, 3
    B. 2, 3, 1, 4
    C. 4, 2, 3, 1
    D. 4, 3, 2, 1

3. Read the following sentences.
    1. The accurate use of difficult words made Chris appear older than his years.
    2. A love of reading enabled Chris to become a successful writer of espionage bestsellers.
    3. Following the words on the page as his mother read aloud, the young boy learned to read himself.
    4. Reading during every spare minute developed an extensive vocabulary for Chris.

    Determine which order of the following sentences is most logical.
    A. 3, 2, 4, 1
    B. 3, 1, 4, 2
    C. 4, 1, 2, 3
    D. 3, 4, 1, 2

4-5A. Continued

4. Read the following sentences.
    1. Sensing this frustration, the KGB spy approached Martin with an offer of much money for copies of the upcoming plans.
    2. Martin was frustrated by the incompetence of his boss on the missile defense planning committee.
    3. Conscience prevailed, and Martin reported the spy to the authorities.
    4. Torn between patriotism and the lure of the money, Martin spent several sleepless nights.

    Determine which order of the following sentences is most logical.
    A. 1, 3, 2, 4
    B. 2, 1, 3, 4
    C. 2, 1, 4, 3
    D. 1, 4, 3, 2

5. Read the following sentences.
    1. Juanita liked Samuel from the first time they met, but she was too shy to let him know.
    2. Much to her surprise, Samuel called for a second date but joked that there would be no food this time.
    3. She could hardly believe he asked her to go to a movie with him.
    4. At the movie she spilled her drink and popcorn in his lap and thought she would never see him again.

    Determine which order of the following sentences is most logical.
    A. 1, 2, 4, 3
    B. 1, 3, 2, 4
    C. 1, 3, 4, 2
    D. 3, 1, 4, 2

4-6. ANOTHER STRATEGY FOR SEQUENCING IDEAS

Cartoons can be an enjoyable way of developing sequencing skills. Generally, there is a logical progression from frame to frame. Both pictures and words provide clues as to the correct sequence.

TESTING TIP:

Some tests require you to reorder the frames of a cartoon that are out of sequence. To solve this kind of problem, first read the cartoon frames. Then, as you study each frame, look for clues that help you to reorder them. Notice the subtle details indicating time. For example, the position of the sun or moon, hands on a clock, clothing, food that has been half eaten or drinks that are half gone, and other such details can offer you hints as to the proper sequence. You will see that one frame cannot occur until another one has.

4-6A. SEQUENCING IDEAS

Activity: Read the following cartoon frames. As you study them, look for clues that help you to order them. Select the correct sequence from the answer choices.

1.

A. 5-3-1-2-4
B. 1-4-5-2-3
C. 1-2-3-4-5
D. 3-1-4-5-2

© 1997 by John Wiley & Sons, Inc.

A. 2-5-1-4-3
B. 1-5-3-2-4
C. 2-5-1-3-4
D. 2-4-1-5-3

4-7. A STRATEGY FOR COMBINING SENTENCES

In standardized and classroom tests, you are often called upon to combine sentences into one sentence that expresses the ideas most clearly and succinctly. It is important that you can identify the key words that need to be used and eliminate repeated and unnecessary words and phrases.

Example: The child approached the bird's nest.
The mother bluejay screeched at her and dove toward her.
The child screamed.

A. As the child approached the nest, the mother bluejay screeched and dove, causing the child to scream.
B. The child approached the bird's nest and the mother bluejay screeched at her and dove toward her and the child screamed.
C. When the child approached the bird's nest, the bluejay screeched and dove toward her and the child screamed.
D. Approaching the nest screaming, the child made the mother bluejay screech and dive.

Explanation: The correct arrangement in this case is A. In this sentence, all of the important information is included, arranged logically, and written clearly and succinctly. In sentence B, the original sentences are connected with a series of *and*'s. Unnecessary words are repeated and the sentence does not flow smoothly. In sentence C, the introductory phrase is good, but the last two original sentences are unchanged. In sentence D, the information is incorrect.

TESTING TIP:

As you read the original sentences, decide which information is important and must be conveyed in the new sentence. Then determine which words and phrases can be eliminated. Read the choices to be sure all necessary information is included. Finally, look for the use of transitional words to make the sentence clear and succinct.

4-7A. COMBINING SENTENCES

Activity: Read the following sentences. Then choose the lettered sentence that best joins these sentences into one.

1. The car was speeding in the fast lane of the highway.
   The car was passing the other vehicles.
   The car was finally pulled over by the police.
   A. The speeding car that was passing other vehicles was in the fast lane of the highway and pulled over by the police.
   B. Because the car was pulled over by the police, it was speeding in the fast lane of the highway and passed the other vehicles.
   C. Since the car was speeding in the fast lane of the highway and was passing the other vehicles, it was pulled over by the police.
   D. The car was speeding in the fast lane of the highway, the car was passing the other vehicles, and the car was finally pulled over by the police.

2. It was a pouring rain.
   The newly seeded yard was quickly becoming muddy.
   The seed was washing away.
   A. A pouring rain on the newly seeded yard caused mud and the seed to be washed away.
   B. The newly seeded yard was rained on, and the mud caused the seed to be washed away.
   C. Because it was a pouring rain, the newly seeded yard was quickly becoming muddy, and the seed was washing away.
   D. The muddy, newly seeded yard was washing away, and it was a pouring rain.

3. The receiver was in position.
   The pass was aimed perfectly.
   The quarterback did not throw hard enough.
   A. Although the receiver was in position and the pass was aimed perfectly, the quarterback did not throw hard enough.
   B. The receiver was in position, the pass was aimed perfectly, and the quarterback did not throw hard enough.
   C. The in-position receiver did not catch the perfectly aimed pass thrown not hard enough by the quarterback.
   D. Because the receiver was in position, the pass was aimed perfectly and the quarterback did not throw hard enough.

4. The vacation had been planned for several months.
   The vacation was to Yosemite National Park.
   The vacation was enjoyed by all.
   A. The vacation had been planned for several months, and the vacation was to Yosemite National Park, and the vacation was enjoyed by all.
   B. Planned for several months, I enjoyed the vacation to Yosemite National Park.
   C. The vacation to Yosemite National Park had been planned for several months and it was enjoyed by all.
   D. Planned for several months, the vacation to Yosemite National Park was enjoyed by all.

4-7A. Continued

5. Jennifer needs to purchase a gift for this evening's birthday party.
   Jennifer needs to hurry.
   The store closes at 4:30.

   A. Jennifer needs to purchase a gift for this evening's birthday party, she needs to hurry, and the store closes at 4:30.

   B. Because Jennifer needs to purchase a gift for this evening's birthday party and the store closes at 4:30, she needs to hurry.

   C. The store closes at 4:30 because Jennifer needs to purchase a gift for this evening's birthday party, and she must hurry.

   D. Jennifer needs to purchase a gift at a store that closes at 4:30 for this evening's birthday party.

Extension: Write three related sentences that can be combined. Combine them into one well-written sentence. Underline those transition words and/or phrases you used to do this.

4-8. ANOTHER STRATEGY FOR COMBINING SENTENCES

In standardized and classroom tests, you are often called upon to combine sentences into one sentence that expresses the ideas most clearly and succinctly. It is important that you can identify the key words that need to be used and eliminate repeated and unnecessary words and phrases.

Example: The checker at the food register was new on the job.
The checker at the food register was slower than usual.
The customers on the long lines were impatient.

    A.   Because the customers on the long lines were impatient, the checker at the food register was new on the job and slower than usual.
    B.   The checker at the food register was new on the job, the checker at the food register was slower than usual, and the customers on the long lines were impatient.
    C.   Since the checker at the food register was new on the job and slower than usual, the customers on the long lines were impatient.
    D.   The new checker at the food register was slower than usual.

Explanation: The correct arrangement in this case is C. In this sentence, all of the important information is included, arranged logically, and written clearly and succinctly. In sentence B, the original sentences are connected with a series of *and*'s. Unnecessary words are repeated and the sentence does not flow smoothly. In sentence A, the introductory phrase is good, but the last two original sentences are not a logical result of the first phrase. In sentence D, important information has been left out of the sentence.

TESTING TIP:

As you read the original sentences, decide which information is important and must be conveyed in the new sentence. Then determine which words and phrases can be eliminated. Read the choices to be sure all necessary information is included. Finally, look for the use of transitional words to make the sentence clear and succinct.

4-8A. COMBINING SENTENCES

Activity: Read the following sentences. Then choose the lettered sentence that best joins these sentences into one.

1. Pablo enjoyed the party at Christine's home.
   Kiki enjoyed the party at Christine's home.
   I enjoyed the party at Christine's home.
   A. Pablo enjoyed the party at Christine's home, Kiki enjoyed the party at Christine's home, and I enjoyed the party at Christine's home.
   B. Pablo and Kiki enjoyed the party at Christine's home, I enjoyed the party at Christine's home.
   C. Because Pablo and Kiki enjoyed the party at Christine's home, I enjoyed it too.
   D. Pablo, Kiki, and I enjoyed the party at Christine's home.

2. The dessert recipe called for special ingredients.
   Margaret didn't have the necessary ingredients.
   Margaret went to the supermarket.
   A. The dessert recipe called for special ingredients, so Margaret went to the supermarket.
   B. Since the dessert recipe called for special ingredients that Margaret didn't have, she went to the supermarket.
   C. The dessert recipe called for special ingredients that the supermarket didn't have.
   D. The dessert recipe called for special ingredients and Margaret didn't have them, so she went to the supermarket to get them.

3. The worsening weather caused commuters to get home late.
   The storm winds were gale force.
   The sleet and hail were pelting the cars.
   A. The worsening gale-force winds and the sleet and hail caused the commuters to get home late.
   B. The commuters got home late, the storm winds were of gale force, and the sleet and hail were pelting the cars.
   C. Worsening weather conditions caused the commuters to get home late.
   D. Sleet, hail, and gale-force storm winds caused the commuters to get home late.

4. The older home needed many cosmetic changes.
   The walls were freshly painted.
   The home looked better already.
   A. The older home needed many cosmetic changes, the walls were freshly painted, so the home looked better already.
   B. In need of many cosmetic changes, the freshly painted walls made the home look better already.
   C. The walls of the older home were freshly painted.
   D. The older home was freshly painted and it looked better already.

4-8A. Continued

5. The television show was very popular.
   The television show aired on Friday nights.
   The television show featured a well-known comedian.

   A. The television show was very popular, it aired on Friday nights, and featured a well-known comedian.
   B. The well-known comedian was featured on a Friday night show.
   C. A very popular, well-known comedian was featured on a Friday night show.
   D. The show that aired on Friday nights was very popular and featured a well-known comedian.

Extension: Write three related sentences that can be combined. Combine them into one well-written sentence. Underline those transition words and/or phrases you used to do this.

4-9. A STRATEGY FOR USING TRANSITIONAL WORDS AND PHRASES

Transitional words and phrases help the reader to understand the relationship between ideas in a sentence or passage. On a standardized or classroom test, you are sometimes called upon to select an appropriate transitional expression to relate two or more ideas.

Example: _____ it was very hot outside, the girl went inside for a cold drink.
    A. Therefore
    B. Because
    C. Nevertheless
    D. Although

Explanation: The correct choice here is the word *Because*. It effectively explains why the girl went inside. It sets up the relationship of cause and effect. The other choices do not logically relate the two ideas. The word *Therefore* does not logically begin this sentence. The word *therefore* usually signals an effect. Since the first part of this sentence is the cause of the girl's action, the word *therefore* makes no sense.

TESTING TIP:

Try each word in the blank to see whether the word and/or phrase sets up a logical relationship. Transitional words set up specific kinds of relationships. Knowing these can be helpful in test-taking. Below are some specific transitions organized by relationship.

Comparison	Contrast	Cause/Effect	Chronological
similarly	however	therefore	first, second, third
in addition	but	accordingly	afterward
again	nevertheless	as a result	eventually
likewise	on the other hand	since	meanwhile

4-9A. USING TRANSITIONAL WORDS AND PHRASES

Activity: Read the following sentences. Then choose the transitional expression that best fits.

1. _____ having three hours of homework tonight, Jenny also needed to go to her karate class.
   A. Thereupon
   B. Also
   C. Above
   D. Besides

2. Mark practiced his dive for months, _____ before the competition he was sure he had forgotten everything.
   A. finally
   B. but
   C. afterward
   D. moreover

3. _____ of having told a lie, Miscall was not allowed to go to the party.
   A. As a result
   B. Eventually
   C. Then
   D. However

4. _____ it was the hottest day of the summer, the mayor announced a heat advisory.
   A. Above
   B. Presently
   C. Since
   D. However

5. It is raining hard; _____ you should wear a raincoat.
   A. therefore,
   B. since
   C. for example,
   D. also,

6. _____ walking, most babies learn to crawl.
   A. Across
   B. Around
   C. Although
   D. Before

4-9A. Continued

7. _____ the earthquake occurred in a remote location, there were no injuries.
   A. Meanwhile
   B. Therefore
   C. Because
   D. Nearby

8. _____, after missing the target completely three times in a row, John agreed to have his vision tested.
   A. Beyond
   B. Otherwise
   C. Finally
   D. Nearby

9. _____ he was an excellent speller, his carelessness resulted in fourteen spelling errors in his history assignment.
   A. Since
   B. Although
   C. For example,
   D. Now

10. All new students are required to take a course in English grammar. _____ the English teachers are pleased to find an improvement in written work.
    A. As a result,
    B. Then
    C. Otherwise
    D. Again

Extension: Find examples of transitional expressions used in a newspaper or magazine. Cut out the passage, highlight at least five expressions, and indicate the kind of relationship each suggests.

4-10. ANOTHER STRATEGY FOR USING TRANSITIONAL WORDS AND PHRASES

Transitional words and phrases help the reader to understand the relationship between ideas in a sentence or passage. On a standardized or classroom test, you are sometimes called upon to select an appropriate transitional expression to relate two or more ideas.

Example: _____ it was very hot outside, the girl went inside for a cold drink.
           A.   Therefore
           B.   Because
           C.   Nevertheless
           D.   Although

Explanation: The correct choice here is the word *Because*. It effectively explains why the girl went inside. It sets up the relationship of cause and effect. The other choices do not logically relate the two ideas. The word *Therefore* does not logically begin this sentence. The word *therefore* usually signals an effect. Since the first part of this sentence is the cause of the girl's action, the word *therefore* makes no sense.

TESTING TIP:

Try each word in the blank to see whether the word and/or phrase sets up a logical relationship. Transitional words set up specific kinds of relationships. Knowing these can be helpful in test-taking. Below are some specific transitions organized by relationship.

Position	Example	Additional Point	Order of Importance
above	for example	also	furthermore
nearby	for instance	in addition	after that
beyond	in brief	similarly	to begin with

4-10A. USING TRANSITIONAL WORDS AND PHRASES

Activity: Read the following sentences. Then choose the transitional expression that best fits.

1. I have given three good reasons to defeat this suggestion. _____ I can offer three more.
   A. On the contrary,
   B. Nearby,
   C. For example,
   D. In addition,

2. The knight saw the silver cup fall from the villain's hand. _____ he seized the cup and rode swiftly to the castle.
   A. Besides,
   B. Beyond,
   C. Thereupon,
   D. For example,

3. Pat watched her older cousin who was painting in the kitchen. _____ Pat asked her parents for a painting set.
   A. After that,
   B. Similarly,
   C. To sum up,
   D. First,

4. Matthew tried his best to win the tennis championship. _____ he practiced his serve every day.
   A. Then
   B. For example,
   C. Beyond,
   D. Otherwise,

5. _____ she was only in seventh grade, people often thought she was older.
   A. Even though
   B. For example,
   C. In fact,
   D. Also,

6. _____ the planet Pluto, there may be another planet called Planet X.
   A. Further
   B. Also
   C. Beyond
   D. Therefore

4-10A. Continued

7. I believe children watch too much television. _____ I can prove this by many surveys showing that many children watch more than 20 hours each week.

    A. Thereafter,
    B. Again,
    C. Nearby,
    D. Furthermore,

8. There are many different ways to draw a tree. _____ you can begin with the trunk and limbs.

    A. On the contrary,
    B. Nearby,
    C. For example,
    D. In addition,

9. The thief ran out of the bank grasping a sack filled with money. _____ the guards came out in hot pursuit.

    A. For instance,
    B. Furthermore,
    C. Next,
    D. Above,

10. Dad just washed the kitchen floor. _____ take off your shoes if you want to go inside.

    A. Therefore,
    B. Otherwise,
    C. Also,
    D. For example,

Extension: Find examples of transitional expressions used in a newspaper or magazine. Cut out the passage, highlight at least five expressions, and indicate the kind of relationship each suggests.

WRITING SAMPLES & OPEN-ENDED RESPONSES

Standardized and classroom tests often use similar vocabulary when presenting test questions and directions. Familiarity with these words and phrasings can be helpful when taking such tests. Increased understanding of these words and phrases will help you in responding to such test questions.

Here is a common direction used on tests specific to writing samples and open-ended reponses:

- Choose the sentence that best states the idea.

4-11. A STRATEGY FOR WRITING YOUR ESSAY RESPONSE

Essay tests are intended to evaluate your knowledge, your ability to analyze and evaluate, and your ability to communicate effectively. In order to insure that you are successful in such essay testing situations, there are strategies you can use to help.

Knowing Your Purpose

1. Read the directions/prompt carefully.

2. Underline key words within the directions/prompt that will help you recognize your goal in writing this essay. Look for words such as those below:

Compare and / or contrast . . .
Explain the causes and / or effects of . . .
Explain the relationship between . . .
Note the sequence of events leading up to . . .
Define or explain the meaning of . . .
Identify possible solutions for a given problem . . .
State your opinion and offer support for your view . . .

Planning Your Response

3. Decide on the best method for organizing your ideas. Consider those prewriting strategies that you find helpful: web, outline, list of key words, word map.

4. Jot down and organize your ideas.

5. Revisit the essay question/prompt. Check to see that your notes respond to the question directly and include all of its parts.

6. Review your notes and determine the sequence you will use to organize the essay.

Knowing the Criteria for Success

7. As you plan to write the essay, keep in mind the following essential elements of good writing:

responsiveness to the topic
organization of ideas
sufficient details and examples
clear introduction, body, and conclusion
content and style that engages the reader
effective vocabulary
legibility

Writing the Essay

8. A strong introductory paragraph is important. A useful structure opens with a generalized statement about the topic. Follow with a sentence about your particular focus of the topic. Then give an overview of what you will present in the paper.

9. The body paragraph(s) should include explanation, details, and examples to develop your response to the topic.

10. Your concluding paragraph should summarize the key points of the essay without presenting new information. It can also evaluate the ideas presented or predict future events.

Proofreading Your Essay

11. Proofread your essay for the following and check each item you have addressed.

Essay Proofreading Checklist

— Essay responds directly and completely to the topic/question/prompt.
— Essay is organized with a clear beginning, middle, and end.
— The first paragraph introduces the topic.
— The body of the essay adequately develops the topic through examples, details, and explanation.
— The conclusion summarizes the essay and ends purposefully.
— This essay uses information and style that will be interesting and informative for the reader.
— Transitional words/phrases logically connect ideas in the essay.
— Vocabulary is varied and appropriate.
— Spelling, mechanics, and usage are correct.
— The essay is legible.

4-12. A STRATEGY FOR WRITING A COMPARISON-AND-CONTRAST ESSAY

The comparison-and-contrast essay requires the writer to explain similarities and/or differences between two given subjects. In this format the writer must recognize these similarities/differences and present them in an organized way. Often the writer will draw conclusions based on these similarities and differences.

Activity: Select one of the following topics for your comparison-and-contrast essay. Using worksheet 4-11, compose an essay that is responsive to the topic you select. The proofreading checklist and a listing of common comparison-and-contrast transitions are included below for your reference.

Topics: Compare and contrast your experiences on a vacation day with your experiences on a typical school day.

There are new experiences awaiting individuals. Some people are more apt to accept the challenges with which they are faced. Some people search for challenges. Identify two individuals who have excelled in their efforts to meet their challenges. One person should be an historical figure and the other should be a present-day figure. Compare and contrast these two individuals.

Compare and contrast a butterfly to a hummingbird.

Transitions: similarly, likewise, however, on the other hand, in addition, again, but, nevertheless

---

Essay Proofreading Checklist

— Essay responds directly and completely to the topic/question/prompt.
— Essay is organized with a clear beginning, middle, and end.
— The first paragraph introduces the topic.
— The body of the essay adequately develops the topic through examples, details, and explanation.
— The conclusion summarizes the essay and ends purposefully.
— This essay uses information and style that will be interesting and informative for the reader.
— Transitional words/phrases logically connect ideas in the essay.
— Vocabulary is varied and appropriate.
— Spelling, mechanics, and usage are correct.
— The essay is legible.

4-13. A STRATEGY FOR WRITING A CAUSE-AND-EFFECT ESSAY

The cause-and-effect essay requires the writer to identify the cause of an event and/or how the event may affect other things. In this format the writer must recognize these causes and effects and present them in an organized way. Often the writer will draw conclusions based on the cause-and-effect relationship. Also the writer may need to make predictions about the effects.

Activity: Select one of the following topics for your cause-and-effect essay. Using worksheet 4-11, compose an essay that is responsive to the topic you select. The proofreading checklist and a listing of common cause-and-effect transitions are included below for your reference.

Topics: Imagine yourself as an author of children's books. Recently, this lucrative field has earned staggering amounts for young authors. What would be the effects of your bestseller earning you one million dollars? Be sure to explain how you earned the one million dollars and how it will affect you.

Telephone communication is something that many people take for granted. Imagine that a worldwide catastrophe occurred eliminating telephone communication for three weeks. What effect would this have on you personally?

Americans have become increasingly more aware of their environment and the need for recycling. Identify those causes leading to mandatory recycling in many communities.

Transitions: therefore, accordingly, as a result, because, since, consequently, hence

---

Essay Proofreading Checklist
— Essay responds directly and completely to the topic/question/prompt.
— Essay is organized with a clear beginning, middle, and end.
— The first paragraph introduces the topic.
— The body of the essay adequately develops the topic through examples, details, and explanation.
— The conclusion summarizes the essay and ends purposefully.
— This essay uses information and style that will be interesting and informative for the reader.
— Transitional words/phrases logically connect ideas in the essay.
— Vocabulary is varied and appropriate.
— Spelling, mechanics, and usage are correct.
— The essay is legible.

Name_____ **Date**_____

4-14. A STRATEGY FOR WRITING AN EXPLANATORY ESSAY

An explanatory essay requires the writer to identify and discuss how two or more ideas/things are related. In this format the writer must recognize the relationship and present it in an organized way.

Activity: Select one of the following topics for your explanatory essay. Using worksheet 4-11, compose an essay that is responsive to the topic you select. The proofreading checklist is included below for your reference.

Topics: Increasingly in our world, children make purchases. Explain the relationship between a child consumer and his or her source of spending money.

In modern times sports has taken on an important role in our society. Explain the relationship between children and sports.

The ocean community is inhabited by a wide variety of organisms. Explain the relationships among creatures of the coral reef.

Essay Proofreading Checklist
— Essay responds directly and completely to the topic/question/prompt.
— Essay is organized with a clear beginning, middle, and end.
— The first paragraph introduces the topic.
— The body of the essay adequately develops the topic through examples, details, and explanation.
— The conclusion summarizes the essay and ends purposefully.
— This essay uses information and style that will be interesting and informative for the reader.
— Transitional words/phrases logically connect ideas in the essay.
— Vocabulary is varied and appropriate.
— Spelling, mechanics, and usage are correct.
— The essay is legible.

4-15. A STRATEGY FOR WRITING A DEFINITION ESSAY

The definition essay requires the writer to explain a term, concept, or process. In this format the writer must recognize the characteristics that distinguish the term, concept, or process from others and present them in an organized way.

Activity: Select one of the following topics for your definition essay. Using worksheet 4-11, compose an essay that is responsive to the topic you select. The proofreading checklist is included below for your reference.

Topics:

The rise of computer and other technological advances has given birth to a new word: *technophobe*. Define the term *technophobe*. Explain how this person is different from others and offer information about his or her behavior and how *technophobia* affects his or her life.

America prides itself on its tradition of individual freedom. The Revolutionary War was fought in the name of liberty. Define and explain freedom from your personal perspective.

Water is essential to life. Our limited supply of water provides a continuing supply through the water cycle. Define and explain how the processes of evaporation and condensation occur in the water cycle.

Essay Proofreading Checklist
— Essay responds directly and completely to the topic/question/prompt.
— Essay is organized with a clear beginning, middle, and end.
— The first paragraph introduces the topic.
— The body of the essay adequately develops the topic through examples, details, and explanation.
— The conclusion summarizes the essay and ends purposefully.
— This essay uses information and style that will be interesting and informative for the reader.
— Transitional words/phrases logically connect ideas in the essay.
— Vocabulary is varied and appropriate.
— Spelling, mechanics, and usage are correct.
— The essay is legible.

4-16. A STRATEGY FOR WRITING A PROBLEM-AND-SOLUTION ESSAY

The problem-and-solution essay requires the writer to identify and explain a given problem and propose solutions to resolve it. In this format the writer must consider various solutions and evaluate both their feasibility and potential effectiveness and present them in an organized way. In this essay form, the conclusion often will contain the best recommendation for solving the problem.

Activity: Select one of the following topics for your problem-and-solution essay. Using worksheet 4-11, compose an essay that is responsive to the topic you select. The proofreading checklist is included below for your reference.

Topics: A twelve-foot nocturnal snake has escaped from a local pet shop in your neighborhood. This elusive creature has terrorized the neighborhood and to date has eaten 8 hamsters, 5 gerbils, and a ferret. The pet store is offering a reward for the safe return of the snake. State the problem clearly and offer at least three strategies for the safe capture of the snake.

A local convenience store, popular with kids in the neighborhood, has been experiencing more and more shoplifting. It appears that candy, magazines, trading cards, and other small items have been taken from the shelves. The owners fear that they may have to close the store if they are unable to stem the tide of theft. Because of the popularity of this store with so many kids, you and your friends have sought to help. Identify the problem in this case and offer at least three strategies to help solve the problem.

Outside your home is a bird feeder. For years, only the birds ate from this feeder. Most recently, however, a family of squirrels has taken over and devoured the food supply. How can you discourage the squirrels from eating your bird seed while continuing to feed the birds?

Essay Proofreading Checklist

— Essay responds directly and completely to the topic/question/prompt.
— Essay is organized with a clear beginning, middle, and end.
— The first paragraph introduces the topic.
— The body of the essay adequately develops the topic through examples, details, and explanation.
— The conclusion summarizes the essay and ends purposefully.
— This essay uses information and style that will be interesting and informative for the reader.
— Transitional words/phrases logically connect ideas in the essay.
— Vocabulary is varied and appropriate.
— Spelling, mechanics, and usage are correct.
— The essay is legible.

4-17. A STRATEGY FOR WRITING AN OPINION ESSAY

The opinion essay requires the writer to analyze both sides of an issue and offer a personal opinion. In this format the writer must recognize both sides of an issue and evaluate both sides before drawing conclusions. The writer must state his or her thoughts and support the view stated.

Activity: Select one of the following topics for your opinion essay. Using worksheet 4-11, compose an essay that is responsive to the topic you select. The proofreading checklist is included below for your reference.

Topics: Recently, your community has experienced a dramatic increase in population. In order to house the many new people in town, the town council has voted to approve a plan to build houses and apartments on the existing sports fields and picnic grounds. Local residents are upset and want to keep the ball fields. Present both sides of this issue and then state your opinion on the matter.

Parents at a local middle school have agreed to limit their children's television viewing time to one hour per day. What is your opinion on this matter? Be sure to state both sides of this issue.

Should scientists experiment with DNA to recreate living dinosaurs?

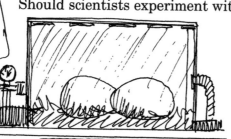

DINOSAUR EGGS
DO NOT DISTURB

Essay Proofreading Checklist
— Essay responds directly and completely to the topic/question/prompt.
— Essay is organized with a clear beginning, middle, and end.
— The first paragraph introduces the topic.
— The body of the essay adequately develops the topic through examples, details, and explanation.
— The conclusion summarizes the essay and ends purposefully.
— This essay uses information and style that will be interesting and informative for the reader.
— Transitional words/phrases logically connect ideas in the essay.
— Vocabulary is varied and appropriate.
— Spelling, mechanics, and usage are correct.
— The essay is legible.

Answer Key

SECTION 2: READING VOCABULARY

2-1A. Recognizing Analogies

1. B
2. C
3. C
4. C
5. D
6. A
7. B
8. D
9. D
10. C

2-1B. Recognizing Analogies

1. D
2. B
3. C
4. C
5. B
6. C
7. A
8. D
9. A
10. B

Sentences will vary.

2-2A. Recognizing Relationships in Analogies

1. B; intensity or size
2. D; intensity
3. B; position
4. A; cause/effect
5. A; youth/adult
6. A; size
7. B; whole/part
8. A; cause/effect
9. C; intensity
10. C; location

Sentences will vary.

2-3A. Recognizing Relationships in Analogies

1. brush; tool/function
2. home; role
3. bank; function
4. poor; opposite
5. cure; function
6. book; creator/medium
7. woods; synonym
8. fish; kind within category
9. repairs; function
10. envelope; packaging

Sentences will vary.

2-4A. Recognizing Synonyms

1. A
2. B
3. D
4. A
5. D
6. D
7. C
8. D
9. B
10. D

Sentences will vary.

2-4B. Recognizing Synonyms

1. A
2. C
3. A
4. A
5. D
6. B
7. C
8. A
9. D
10. C

Sentences will vary.

2-5A. Recognizing Synonyms
1. B
2. B
3. A
4. A
5. A
6. D
7. C
8. C
9. A
10. B

2-6A. Recognizing Antonyms
1. D
2. C
3. C
4. A
5. B
6. D
7. B
8. B
9. A
10. B

Sentences will vary.

2-7A. Recognizing Antonyms
1. C
2. D
3. B
4. C
5. C
6. B
7. A
8. B
9. A
10. C

2-8A. Determining Vocabulary in Context
1. B
2. A

3. C
4. B
5. C
6. D
7. B
8. D
9. A
10. C

2-9A. Determining Vocabulary in Context (Challenge Level)
1. C
2. C
3. B
4. C
5. B
6. A
7. B
8. B
9. C
10. D

2-10A. Determining Vocabulary in Context
1. D
2. D
3. A
4. D
5. B
6. A
7. D
8. B
9. D
10. D

2-11A. Taking In-class Tests
1. *(sample)* geometric shape
closed figure; four equal sides
study of geometry

The square is a geometric, closed figure shape with four equal sides.
Squares can be found in the field of

geometry and can be observed in many aspects of our environment.

2-5. *See above sample.*

2-11B. Taking In-class Tests
1-5. See sample given for 2-11A.

2-12A. Writing Sentences That Show Understanding
1. *(sample)* The litter and trash that cover the sides of the highway further pollute our environment.

2-5. *See above sample.*

2-12B. Writing Sentences That Show Understanding
1-5. See sample given in 2-12A.

2-13A. Taking Multiple-Choice Tests
1. C
2. D
3. A
4. B
5. B

2-14A. Taking Matching Tests
1. E
2. D
3. F
4. G
5. H
6. C
7. A
8. B

2-15A. Taking Fill-in-the-Blank Tests
1. Washington, D.C.
2. Michigan, Erie, Huron, Ontario, Superior *(in any order)*
3. Rhode Island
4. Georgia, Alabama, Louisiana *(in any order)*
5. Washington, California, Oregon *(in any order)*
6. Helena

7. Arizona
8. Wyoming
9. Utah

2-16A. Decoding Dinosaurs
1. armed lizard
2. thunder lizard
3. helmeted lizard
4. terrible lizard
5. bird imitator
6. thick-headed lizard
7. first horn-faced lizard
8. egg thief

2-17A. Decoding Unfamiliar Words
1. against abortion
   against bacteria
   against freezing
   against
2. together
3. self
4. former
5. earth
6. not
7. not
8. again
9. across
10. between
Definitions will vary.

2-17B. Decoding Unfamiliar Words
1. proper, correct
2. half, not fully
3. God or a god
4. fictitious; counterfeit
5. before
6. four
7. repeat
8. three
9. man, human
10. opposite; away
Definitions will vary.

2-18A. Decoding Unfamiliar Words

1. capable of
2. filled with
3. having
4. without
5. behavior characteristic
6. state or condition
7. study of
8. having the characteristic of
9. state or condition
10. quality or state

Definitions will vary.

COMPREHENSION

2-19A. Identifying the Main Idea

1. C
2. B

2-20A. Identifying the Main Idea

1. Hercules was an intelligent, strong, and courageous Greek hero known for successfully facing great challenges.
2. In 1780 Benedict Arnold, a well-respected patriot in the colonial army and convinced by his bride that the British's cause was right, turned traitor and gave the British a chance to capture West Point.

2-21A. Organizing Information

*The semantic maps will vary but all have **Spider** as the center of the map.*

2-22A. Organizing Information

*The semantic maps will vary but all have **Celestial Objects** as the center of the map.*

2-23A. Organizing Information

This map will show the sequence of events in the eruption of Mount St. Helens in 1980 and how one event caused the next.

2-24A. Sequencing Ideas

1. C
2. C
3. C
4. D
5. B

2-25A. Sequencing Ideas

1. D
2. A
3. C

2-26A. Drawing Conclusions

1. C
2. C
3. C
4. B
5. D

2-27A. Drawing Conclusions

1. D
2. B
3. A
4. D
5. C

2-28A. Recognizing Author's Style

1. C
2. B
3. B
4. "This must stop!"
5. "Unsupervised television viewing prevents children from developing their minds and bodies."
6. "American children are not taking to the playgrounds as they have in the past."

SECTION 3: LANGUAGE SPELLING

3-1A. Proofreading to Find Errors

1. C
2. D

3. B
4. D
5. D
6. D
7. A
8. B
9. D
10. B

3-1B. Proofreading to Find Errors

1. B
2. B
3. C
4. C
5. A
6. D
7. D
8. C
9. A
10. C

3-2A. Proofreading to Find Homonym Errors

1. C
2. A
3. D
4. A
5. D
6. D
7. A
8. D
9. A
10. A

3-3A. Proofreading to Find the Error

1. B
2. D
3. B
4. C

5. C
6. B
7. A
8. D
9. D
10. A

3-3B. Proofreading to Find the Error

1. C
2. C
3. B
4. A
5. A
6. D
7. B
8. D
9. B
10. C

3-4A. Proofreading to Find the Error

1. B
2. A
3. D
4. C
5. B
6. C
7. A
8. D
9. C
10. A

3-4B. Proofreading to Find the Error

1. B
2. C
3. D
4. B
5. C

6. A

7. A

8. D

9. D

10. A

3-5A. Recognizing Correct Spelling

1. C

2. C

3. C

4. D

5. B

6. D

7. C

8. B

9. D

10. A

3-5B. Recognizing Correct Spelling

1. D

2. D

3. C

4. B

5. D

6. A

7. D

8. B

9. C

10. B

MECHANICS AND USAGE

3-6A. Identifying Capitalization Errors

1. C

2. B

3. C

4. A

5. A

6. B

7. A

8. B

9. A

10. A

3-7A. Identifying Correct Capitalization

1. A

2. C

3. A

4. A

5. B

6. B

7. B

8. A

9. B

10. B

3-8A. Identifying Punctuation Errors

1. A

2. B

3. B

4. C

5. A

6. D

7. D

8. A

9. D

10. B

11. D

12. A

13. D

14. C

15. D

3-8B. Identifying Punctuation Errors

1. A

2. D

3. C

4. B

5. B
6. A
7. B
8. D
9. C
10. B

3-9A. Identifying Correct Punctuation

1. B
2. C
3. C
4. A
5. A
6. C
7. B
8. D
9. D
10. A
11. C
12. D
13. C
14. A
15. D

3-10A. Identifying Usage Errors

1. A
2. B
3. A
4. A
5. D
6. A
7. B
8. A
9. B
10. A

3-11A. Identifying Correct Usage

1. C
2. C

3. D
4. A
5. C
6. D
7. D
8. A
9. A
10. B

SECTION 4: WRITING COMPOSITION

4-1A. Selecting the Topic Sentence

1. A
2. D
3. B
4. C
5. A

4-2A. Writing Topic Sentences
Answers will vary.

4-3A. Selecting Supporting Details

1. C
2. B
3. B
4. A
5. C

4-4A. Selecting Supporting Details

1. D
2. A
3. B
4. A
5. B
6. C
7. C
8. B
9. C

4-5A. Sequencing Ideas

1. B
2. C

3. D
4. C
5. C

4-6A. Sequencing Ideas
1. B
2. D

4-7A. Combining Sentences
1. C
2. C
3. A
4. D
5. B

4-8A. Combining Sentences
1. D
2. B
3. D
4. B
5. D

4-9A. Using Transitional Words and Phrases
1. D
2. B
3. A

4. C
5. A
6. D
7. C
8. C
9. B
10. A

4-10A. Using Transitional Words and Phrases
1. D
2. C
3. A
4. B
5. A
6. C
7. D
8. C
9. C
10. A

WRITING SAMPLES & OPEN-ENDED RESPONSES

4-11 through 4-17. *Answers will vary.*

NOTES

NOTES

NOTES

NOTES

NOTES

NOTES

NOTES

NOTES

NOTES